New ENGLISH CONNECTIONS

Developing English Fluency

4

Young & Son Global, Inc.

Syllabus

Title		Functions	Language Focus
Unit 1 Small Talk	p.4	Making introductions and small talk	*so, too, either, neither*
Unit 2 Career Changes	p.8	Discussing career decisions and changes	Present perfect continuous
Unit 3 Self-Help	p.12	Sharing ideas about good and bad habits	*used to* + verb vs. *be/get used to* + *-ing*
Unit 4 Sports & Leisure	p.16	Talking about leisure locations and activities	Gerunds as subjects and objects
Unit 5 The Perfect Match	p.20	Exchanging ideas about suitable partners	*want, hope, wish* (+ infinitive or *that*-clause)
Unit 6 New Products	p.24	Discussing new consumer products	*It looks* (*sounds/smells/tastes/feels*) + adjective vs. *It looks like* + noun
Unit 7 Urban Legends	p.28	Talking about urban legends and conspiracy theories	Reported speech
Unit 8 Prejudice	p.32	Discussing first impressions and prejudice	*all, some, most, many, a few, no(none)* (+ *of*)
Unit 9 In The News	p.36	Talking about news / media sources	Passive voice
Unit 10 Helping Out	p.40	Exchanging ideas and opinions about volunteering	Non-referential *it* and *there*
Unit 11 Friendship	p.44	Talking about friends and friendship	Phrasal verbs using *break, call,* and *do*
Unit 12 Lookism	p.48	Talking about beauty and its role in workplace relations	Stative verbs of cognition

Pronunciation or Talk Tips	Listening	Communication
Expressions with *up*	Three people making small talk and introductions	Getting to know your classmates
Content word stress	Three people discussing their career changes	Role play – making career changes
Expressions related to feelings	Three people talking about their problems at a self-help meeting	*Find someone who* ... activity about habits
Idiomatic expressions for sports scores	A radio talk show about leisure preferences	Planning sports-related vacations
Consonant blending – silent, blended final *t*	A conversation of a couple – "Breaking up is hard to do."	Group discussions – "A time for change"
Idioms related to *likes* and *dislikes*	Three different TV commercials	Creating a new consumer product and presenting a commercial
Changes in consonant clusters	A conversation between a stranger and a student about conspiracies	Describing and creating urban legends or conspiracy theories
Idioms of confusion and mistakes	A conversation between two people about making snap judgments	Group discussions – "A few good men"
Idioms of self-control	A news report about a trial of a "famous" actor	Creating and presenting your own TV news broadcast
Syllable stress in words with *-tion* suffixes	Radio interviews about community volunteer work	Survey – "What kind of volunteer are you?"
Proverbs related to friendship	Three people speaking about their friendships	Making a questionnaire – "What kind of friend are you?"
Proverbs related to beauty and appearance	Three talk-show guests discussing "lookism" in the workplace	Group discussion – "Who looks good for the job?"

UNIT 1 Small Talk

Warm Up

How to make small talk

A. Fill in the blanks with a suitable word or expression. Check your answers with a partner.

1. What an _awful_ day!
2. Is this your first trip to ________?
3. Have you seen ________ yet?
4. It's really ________, isn't it?
5. What did you ________ on your vacation?
6. Did you ________ the earthquake?
7. I like your ________. Where did you get them?
8. Any ________ for the weekend?
9. How was your ________?
10. How's ________ going?

B. *Pair work* **Match the responses below to the small talk questions in part A.**

a. You can say that again. _1_
b. No. What happened? ____
c. Oh, thanks. I'm not sure. They were a gift. ____
d. I went to the beach. How about you? ____
e. Oh, I know. ____
f. I'm not too sure yet. You? ____
g. You know, same as always. Yourself? ____
h. It was fine, I slept the entire time. ____
i. No, but I'm hoping to soon. Is it good? ____
j. No, I've been here before. ____

Listening

Don't I know you? T02

A. Listen and answer the following questions. Check your answers with a partner.

1. How do Ben and Craig know each other?
2. What are they both trying to do right now?
3. How does Craig know Lucy? How does Ben feel about meeting her?
4. What does Lucy suggest to Ben? What's Ben's response?

B. *Pair work* Ask and answer the following questions with a partner.

1. What kinds of things do you talk about at parties?
2. Do you ever talk to people you don't know?
   If so, what do you say? If not, why?
3. What are some other situations where you make small talk?
4. Has a stranger ever started a conversation with you?
   What did they talk about?

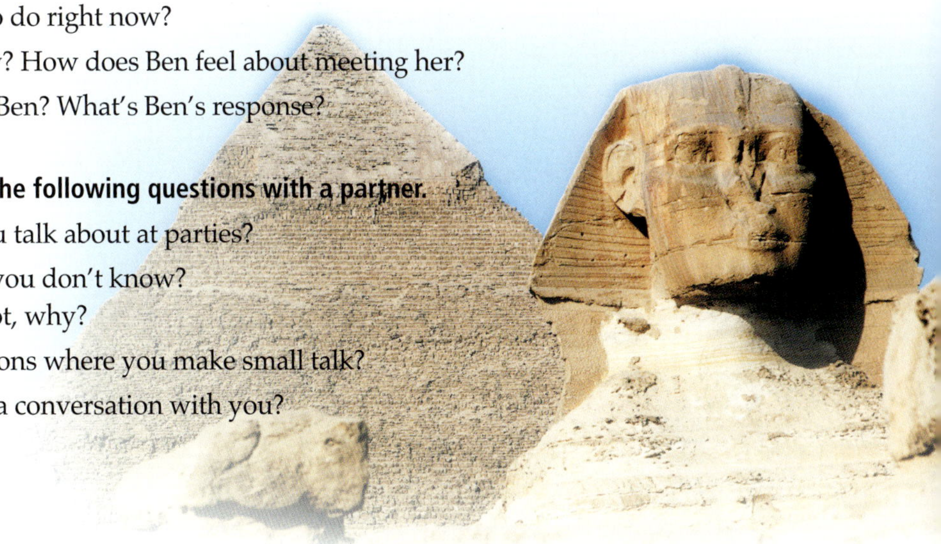

Talk Tips

Expressions with *up*

A. Read the following expressions with *up*. What does each one mean?

What are you **up** to these days?	What's **up**?
Things are looking **up**.	What did you get **up** to?

B. *Pair work* Match the expressions (1 – 5) with their definitions on the right (a – e). Check your answers with a partner.

1. What time did you show up last night?
2. Are you up to going?
3. It's difficult for me to open up.
4. It's up to you.
5. I used up all my credit yesterday.

a. Do you feel like going?
b. When did you arrive?
c. It's your decision.
d. There's no time left on my phone card.
e. I find it hard to express how I feel easily.

C. *Pair work* Use expressions with *up* from parts A and B to make a question (Q) or to respond to a comment (R). Role-play each situation with a partner.

1. You want to quit studying English. (R)
2. It's early on a Monday morning. (Q)
3. You have a problem. (R)
4. You want to play tennis this afternoon. You need a partner. (Q)

Language Focus

so / too / either / neither

A. With a partner, ask and answer the questions below.

QUESTIONS	ANSWERS
I have to find a new job. I really love traveling. I need to study. I play soccer on weekends.	Me **too**. **So** do I. I do, **too**.
I'm studying English on Sundays now. I went backpacking in Europe in college. I can speak a little French. I'll take the TOEIC next month.	**So** am I. I did, **too**. **So** can I. I will, **too**.
I don't like that show. I don't know anyone at this party. I don't know how to swim. I don't have a driver's license.	Me **neither**. **Neither** do I. I don't, **either**.
I'm not going to the party. I didn't study Chinese in school. I can't speak Japanese. I won't do that again.	**Neither** am I. I didn't, **either**. **Neither** can I. I won't, **either**.

B. *Pair work* Fill in the blanks with your own information. Read out your statements to your partner. Agree or disagree with each other and ask follow-up questions.

I like ____________ on the weekend.

I can ______________ very well.

I have never seen ___________.

I am hoping to ___________ sometime this year.

I thought school/college was ___________.

I ___________ gambling.

I don t know how to ___________.

I m planning to ______________ tonight.

I like hiking on the weekend.

So do I. Where do you like to hike?

I like hiking in the mountains.

Communication

A lot in common

A. **Fill in the information below and then compare your answers with a partner.**

Yourself		*Your partner*
	The last movie you saw	
	A famous person you have met	
	A hobby or sport that you are interested in	
	A club or group you are a member of	
	The last CD or DVD you bought	
	A foreign country you have visited	*Egypt*
	How long have you studied here	
	Something you can do well	

B. ***Group work*** **Imagine you are at a party. Introduce your partner to another pair using some of the information above.**

I'd like to introduce you to a friend of mine. This is Jose.

It's good to meet you, Jose.

It's good to meet you, too.

Jose just came back from Egypt.

C. ***Class work*** **Walk around the class and try to gather as much of the information about your classmates as you can. When you have finished, complete the information in the box and compare with your group.**

1. Three adjectives that describe you
2. A famous person that you don't like
3. A place you would like to visit
4. Something you would like to be famous for
5. A famous person you would like to go out to dinner with
6. Something you would like to give up / take up
7. A food you can't stand
8. A TV drama that you loved / hated
9. A book you really enjoyed
10. Something you can't do but wish you could do

I'm ________ and so is ________.

I'm not ________ and neither is ________.

I like ________ and ________ does, too.

I can't stand ________ and neither can ________.

I would never ________ and ________ wouldn't, either.

I would like to try ________ and so would ________.

I would love to be famous for ________ and ________ would, too.

I want to visit ________ and so does ________.

I can't ________ and neither can ________.

UNIT 2 Career Changes

Warm Up

Tell me what you really want to do!

A. **What changes do you think the following people should make to their lives? Write a suggestion for each person in the blanks below. Compare your answers with a partner.**

I work in a big city, but I'm happiest when camping. You need a university education for most of the jobs I'd like to have. I wish I had gone to university.

He *should quit his job and go back to school. He should study to become a park ranger.*

I want to have my own business. I hate living in the city. I like books, art, and relaxing with friends in coffee shops.

She ____________________

I work for an advertising company but I'm not happy. People say that I have a gift for artistic work, and I also like computers.

She ____________________

I got involved in my family's business, but that was never my dream. I like cooking and writing.

He ____________________

B. ***Pair work*** **Ask and answer the following questions with a partner.**

1. Why might some people become unhappy with their careers?
2. Do you know anyone who changed their career, or their university major? Give details.
3. Do people switch jobs or change careers more often these days? Explain.
4. Who do you usually get advice from when you make career decisions? Why?

Listening

New directions

T03

A. Listen and answer the following questions. Check your answers with a partner.

1. What did Jason do before quitting his job? Why did he quit? What does he do now?
2. How did Diane feel in her old job? Why is she happier where she is now?
3. Why did William quit his job? What is he doing now?
4. How does William's wife feel about the change?

B. *Pair work* **Ask and answer the following questions with a partner.**

1. Which person's choices do you like the most why?
2. Do you think it was easy for these people to make these changes? Why / Why not?
3. Do you think you could do what these people did? What makes you say so?
4. What big changes would you like to make? Why?

Pronunciation

Content word stress

A. Listen and repeat. Notice which words are stressed in the following sentences. T04

I've *always loved* and wanted to *play* ***music***.
I had *always* wanted to *own* my own ***business***.
It was *stressful* for ***me***.
I *quit* my job as a *taxi* ***driver***.

B. *Pair work* **Fill in the blanks with words or phrases of your choice. Ask your questions and answer your partner's questions using correct word stress.**

1. Why did you ask him about ______________?
2. Are you going to get married ______________?
3. How long have you ____________________?
4. When will you ________________________?

Language Focus
Present perfect continuous

A. With a partner, ask and answer the questions below.

QUESTIONS		ANSWERS	
What **have** you **been doing** these days? What **have** you **been** up to these days?		I've been	**working** a lot. **looking** for a job. **playing** the guitar every day. **studying** English. **doing** a lot of reading.
Have you **been**	**looking** for a new job? **enjoying** the weather these days? **doing** your homework? **working** out lately? **watching** any good shows recently?	Yes, I have. No, I haven't.	
What kind of What sort of What	work **have** you **been doing**? books **have** you **been reading** lately? TV shows **have** you **been watching**? classes **have** you **been taking**?	I**'ve been working** at a bank. I**'ve been reading** a lot of novels. I **haven't been watching** a lot of TV these days. I **haven't been taking** any classes lately.	
How long **have** you **been working** there? Where **have** you **been going** on the weekends? Why **have** you **been studying** so much? Who **have** you **been going** out with lately?		I**'ve been working** here for about a year. I**'ve been visiting** my parents every weekend lately. I have a big test next week. I**'ve been seeing** that girl from accounting.	

B. *Pair work* **Discuss the following with your partner.**

1. What have you been doing a lot of these days?
2. How long have you been at your current job / school?
3. What TV shows have you been watching lately?
4. Have you been enjoying the weather these days? What have you been doing?

Communication

What have you been doing?

A. **Imagine that you have a new job. Answer the questions by filling in the blanks below each picture.**

B. ***Group work*** **Your group will ask you the same questions from part A above. Imagine that you are not happy with your job/major. Answer the questions by using the answers from another student's book.**

> What has been causing you stress? Give details.

> I've been working a lot at my company this year. There were many nights that I had to stay late at work.

C. ***Group work*** **Discuss the unhappy lives from part B above, and decide on a group answer for how these people could be happier. When ready, present your group's ideas to the class.**

> My job is a receptionist in the exercise and my group gave me lots of useful advice. First, they said that I should ...

UNIT

3 Self-Help

Warm Up

Can't help myself!

A. **Which of the habits below are good and which are bad? Match the expressions with the pictures. Check your answers with a partner.**

1. ~~smoking~~
2. biting your nails
3. picking your nose
4. spitting
5. washing your hands
6. eating an apple a day
7. slurping your noodles
8. jiggling your legs
9. popping gum
10. reading
11. hair twirling
12. twirling a pen
13. burping

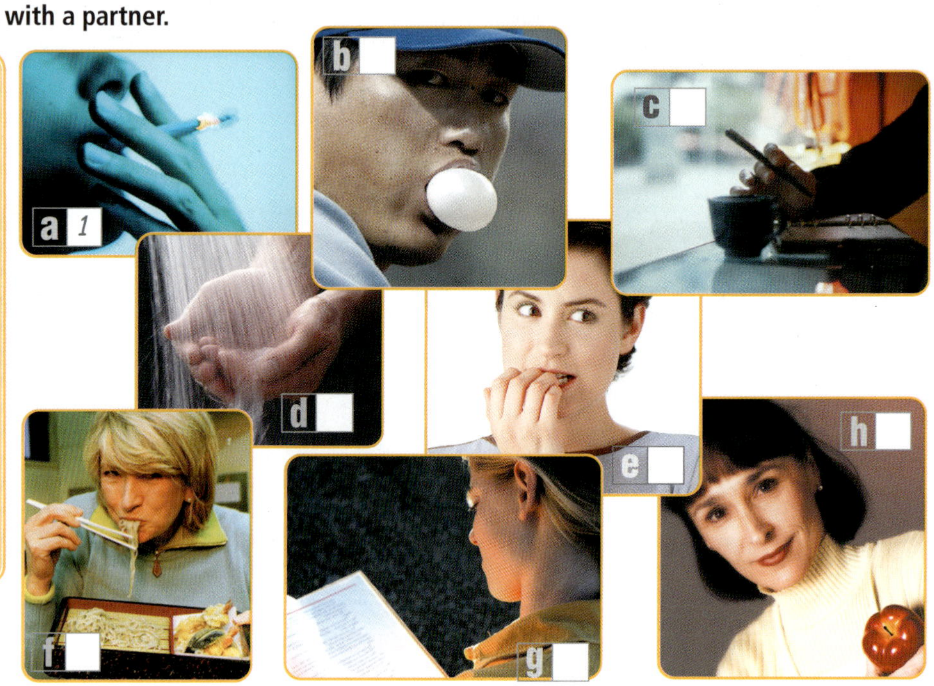

B. *Pair work* **Write two of your good and two of your bad habits below, then discuss them with a partner. Give your partner advice on overcoming their bad habits.**

GOOD

BAD

One of my bad habits is biting my nails. My nails look so ugly.

Maybe you should try doing something with your hands. For example, knitting.

C. *Pair work* **Ask and answer the following questions with a partner.**

1. What other good/bad habits can you think of? Why are they good/bad?
2. Have you ever had any bad habits? What were they? Did you stop?
3. What do you think the worst habit is? Why do you think so?
4. What good habits would you like to start? Why?

Listening

Bad habits anonymous

T05

A. Listen and answer the following questions. Check your answers with a partner.

1. What is Beth's problem? How is she trying to deal with it?
2. What did Dominic's girlfriend tell him about his bad habit?
3. How does Sean feel about sharing his problem?
4. What is Sean afraid of? What happens nowadays when he sees one?

B. *Pair work* Ask and answer the following questions with a partner.

1. Who do you share your problems with? Do they help you? How?
2. What problems do you think people should get professional help for? Why?
3. What are some ways people can stop some of the minor bad habits from the previous page?
4. What do you think about people who go on TV with their problems? Would you ever do that?

Talk Tips

Expressions related to feelings

A. Read the following expressions related to feelings. What does each one mean?

Does the fear of heights always **get to** you?
That was **a hard pill to swallow**.
Do you want to **open up** and share your story?
It's embarrassing **pouring your heart out** to strangers.

B. *Pair work* Complete the sentences with expressions from the box below.

choke up	be/get fed up	get ... off one's chest
get wound up	break out in(to) laughter/tears	burst someone's bubble

1. If you ever feel like ________ your worries ____________, please give me a call anytime.
2. My friend Mike ____________ easily with his silly practical jokes.
3. Up until Emily ____________, Nicholas thought he was the most handsome guy in class.
4. Matt got ____________ telling me about the death of his favorite pet as a young boy.
5. I ____________ when I heard that Jasmine had been diagnosed with cancer.
6. Melanie ____________ with the time it's taking to process her work visa.

C. *Pair work* Ask and answer the following questions with a partner.

1. Who do you generally pour your heart out to? Why that person?
2. What movie or event has caused you to get choked up?
3. Have you ever received any news that was a hard pill to swallow? What happened?
4. When you have a problem with someone, do you get it off your chest by talking to them directly?

Language Focus

used to / be used to / get used to

A. With a partner, ask and answer the questions below.

QUESTIONS		ANSWERS	
Did you **use to** **Didn't** you **use to**	have long hair? work here? live in Chicago? play basketball?	I did. I **used to** have long hair. Yes, I did. No, I've never lived in Chicago. No, I didn't.	
What **did** you **use to** do? Where **did** you **use to** live? What kinds of clothes **did** you **use to** wear? How **did** you **use to** look?		I **used to**	be a teacher. live in London. wear jeans and T-shirts. have really short hair and a beard.
Are you **used to** Have you **gotten used to**	this weather? getting up early? working so hard? eating spicy food?	Yes, I**'m used to** it. I'm slowly **getting used to** it. No, I**'m** not **used to** it yet. No, I can't **get used to** it.	
How have you changed since school? How has she changed since you last saw her? Was it hard to **get used to** working there? What was the hardest thing to **get used to**?		I **used to** sleep in a lot. Now I**'m used to** getting up early. She **used to** be shy. Now she's outgoing and talkative. No, it was easy to **get used to**. I love working there. The hardest thing to **get used to** was the cold weather.	

B. ***Pair work*** **Discuss the following with your partner.**

1. What did you use to be afraid of when you were young? How did you overcome it?
2. What hobbies did you use to have? Why don't you do them nowadays?
3. What is the hardest thing to get used to when you get a new job?
4. What is something you think you'll never get used to? Why do you think so?

Communication

Looking back

A. Write questions below using *used to, be used to,* and *get used to*.

used to	be used to	get used to
1. *Did you use to ride a bike when you were a child?*	1.	1.
2.	2.	2.
3.	3.	3.
4.	4.	4.

B. *Class work* Write your questions from above in the spaces below. Talk to as many class members as you can and write their answers in the spaces. Write one answer per square.

Q A	Q A	Q A
Q Did you use to ride a bike when you were a child? A	Q A	Q A
Q A	Q A	Q A
Q A	Q A	Q A

C. *Class work* Record the information from the squares above onto separate pieces of paper. Do not repeat any information already written.

D. *Group work* Your teacher will give you an information sheet from part C. Form small groups and discuss the information on the sheet.

It says here you used to live in England. How long were you there for?

Well, I moved there with my parents when I was about 15 years old. I had a great time there, but it took a while for me to get used to the different accents.

UNIT

4 Sports & Leisure

Warm Up

You only live once!

A. **Look at the travel ads below and write down the activities you can do in each place. Compare your answers with a partner and discuss the activities you've tried.**

B. ***Pair work*** **Ask and answer the following questions with a partner.**

1. What are some of the recreation hot spots in your country? What do people do there?
2. Do you prefer active vacations or relaxing ones? Why?
3. Have you ever gone anywhere like the places listed above? If so, where? If not, where would you like to go?
4. What is your favorite place to just hang out, relax, and do nothing?

Listening

Putting fun back into your life T06

A. Listen and answer the following questions. Check your answers with a partner.

1. What big change did David make in his life? What does he do now?
2. What are Robert's three great loves?
3. What does Beth do for a living?
4. What does she do in her free time?

B. *Pair work* Ask and answer the following questions with a partner.

1. Which of the three people's lifestyles would you enjoy the most?
2. What sports or activities do you associate with older people?
3. Do you have enough leisure time? If not, why don't you?
4. How else can people put fun back into their lives?

Talk Tips

How to say scores in English

A. Read the following idioms related to sports scores below. What does each one mean?

The Honeybees **narrowly beat** the Hens 6-5.
The Honeybees **won against/beat** the Hens 4-2.
The Honeybees **hammered/whipped/creamed/thrashed** the Hens 11-1.
The Honeybees **tied with/drew with** the Hens 1-1.
The Honeybees **ran away with the game** 7-0.

B. *Pair work* Use the clues above to practice saying the scores below.

SCORES

Honeybees **7**, Hens **6**	Honeybees **2**, Comets **2**
Lions **15**, Honeybees **1**	Honeybees **5**, Wings **3**

C. *Pair work* Imagine that you are hosting a sports radio talk show. Take turns commenting on scores below. Then create your own scores!

Baseball: Gears 19, Rays 3 — Basketball: Cats 87, Force 85
Soccer: Hares 1, Kits 1 — Football: Pilots 42, Wizards 0

In baseball, the Gears creamed the Rays, 19-3.

The Gears just ran away with the game.

Language Focus

Gerunds

A. **With a partner, ask and answer the questions below.**

QUESTIONS			ANSWERS
What do you	like enjoy	doing in your free time? doing on vacation? doing after work? watching on TV?	I like **reading** and **playing** board games. I enjoy **going** to the beach. I like **having** drinks with friends. I like **watching** the news.
What's a good way to What's the best way to		relax? learn English? meet new people? spend my vacation?	**Meditating** is a good way to relax. **Practicing** every day is the best way to learn English. **Joining** a club is a good way to meet people. **Lying** on the beach.
Which do you like more, running or hiking? Which do you like better, reading or watching TV? What causes you a lot of stress? What's the worst thing about studying English?			I like **hiking** more than **running**. I think **reading** is more **relaxing** than **watching** TV. **Meeting** deadlines is really stressful. The worst thing is **memorizing** vocab.
What is your favorite pastime? What is your passion? Why are you so tired? What don't you like about working there?			**Bowling** is my favorite pastime. **Skydiving** is my passion. I'm exhausted from **working** all day. I hate **getting** up early.

B. *Pair work* **Discuss the following with your partner.**

1. What are some things you enjoy doing in your free time? Why do you enjoy them?
2. What are some things you hate doing? Why do you hate them?
3. What activities do you think are relaxing? How often do you do them?
4. What activities do you think are fun or exciting? How often do you do them?

Communication

Sports safaris

A. *Pair work* **Look at the activities and their descriptions below. Add two more activities and then discuss them with a partner. Circle the ones you both like.**

Category	Description	Activities
1. Easy	You usually won't sweat.	Watching sports,
2. Active	You may sweat or get sore muscles.	Playing golf,
3. Athletic	Requires skill and fitness; you'll definitely sweat.	Skiing,
4. Extreme	These are exciting but may be dangerous.	Skydiving,

B. *Pair work* **Rank these two-week long sports vacations in the order of your preference. (1=best) Discuss your rankings with a partner. Then split up and find out the rest of your classmates' preferences.**

Chicago – A Sports Fan's Paradise!

Categories: 1-2
Location: Big city; no mountains, but Lake Michigan is nearby for summer water-sports!
Planned activities: Watching pro sports (baseball, basketball, and football), bowling, playing bingo ($5,000 prizes!), urban hiking (neighborhood tours), gambling on riverboats, and dancing at night are included!
Hot tip: Good skydiving is 2 hours away.
Options: ______________________

Extreme New Zealand – Super Sports Safari!

Categories: 3-4
Location: Far away from the city
Planned activities: Skiing, bungee jumping, boating, fishing, whale watching, swimming with dolphins, skydiving, spelunking (exploring caves), and rock climbing are all here for your enjoyment.
Hot tip: Try "tramping" — that's the Kiwi word for "hiking".
Options: ______________________

Mexico's Baja region – The Surf's Better in Baja!

Categories: 1-4
Location: Warm, dry desert mountains and clear, blue seas
Planned activities: We'll surf, sail, swim, dive, snorkel, and fish. We'll also hike and bike in the desert, drive racing-cars, and ride motorcycles. Tired? Hang out at the pool or play an easy game of golf.
Hot tips: Watching bullfights and boxing matches is very popular!
Options: ______________________

C. *Group work* **Choose a sports vacation and make changes based on your classmates' preferences from parts A and B. If you add an option, you must take away one planned activity. Take turns presenting your new sports vacation to the other groups.**

Why don't we add "playing golf" to the New Zealand trip?

Good idea. Should we take away skiing? None of our classmates like skiing.

UNIT 5 The Perfect Match

Warm Up

Not my type

A. *Pair work* **Decide if any of the things on the list below would turn you off about a possible partner. Rate each one on a scale of 1 – 10 (1 = no problem at all, 10 = a total turn off).**

- Heavy smoker
- A tattoo
- Pierced tongue
- Unfashionable clothes
- Heavy drinker
- Fussy eater
- Strongly religious
- Shaved head
- Emotional
- Serious relationships in the past
- Swears a lot
- Hates to spend money
- Very tall
- Long fingernails
- Very close to their mother
- Hairy legs

How do you feel about pierced tongues?

I rated it 10. I wouldn't even think of going out with someone with a pierced tongue.

B. *Pair work* **Ask and answer the following questions with a partner.**

1. What things other than those above turn you off?
2. Have you ever dated anyone who did or had any of the things from above?
3. What would you do if you discovered something about your partner that you found unattractive?
4. Which qualities do men and women look for when they are looking for a partner?
5. Do you think there really is a difference in the qualities men and women look for in a partner or does it just depend on your style?

Listening

Breaking up is hard to do. T07

A. Listen and answer the following questions. Check your answers with a partner.

1. How long have Helen and Brad been going out?
2. Why is Helen upset? Give a few reasons.
3. When does Helen hope to get married? Is she optimistic? Why / Why not?
4. What are some things she wants to change?

B. *Pair work* Ask and answer the following questions with a partner.

1. Do you know anyone like Brad or Helen? What are they like?
2. What special days are important to you? What would you do if someone forgot them?
3. Do you think people in a relationship can change each other? Why / Why not?
4. What would you be willing to give up in order to save a relationship? What wouldn't you give up?

Pronunciation

Consonant blends

A. Listen and repeat. Notice how the final *t* is dropped or blended into the next word. T08

Last month, you forgot my birthday.	I want someone who is considerate.
You didn't even get me a card.	I wish you wouldn't drink so much.
I can't remember everything.	It's the most difficult thing I've ever done.

B. *Pair work* Complete the sentences below with information about yourself. Compare your sentences with a partner.

1. The most difficult thing about a relationship is ...
2. I wish my partner wouldn t ...
3. I want my partner to be more ...
4. Sometimes I forget to ...
5. In the next five years, I plan to ...
6. In the last few years/months, ...

I want my partner to be more outgoing. She's so shy.

What's the problem?

Language Focus
want / hope / wish

A. With a partner, ask and answer the questions below.

QUESTIONS		ANSWERS	
What do you **want**?		I **want**	a good relationship.
What do you **want**	in a partner?		someone who will love me.
	to do in the future?		to find my soul mate.
	me to do?		you to help me.
What do you **hope** for?		I **hope**	for a happy ending.
What do you **hope**	for in life?		(that) I have children and grandchildren.
	to do in the near future?		to get married soon.
	happens?		(that) things work out.
What do you **wish** for?		I **wish**	for a good marriage.
What do you **wish**	you could do?		I could see her again.
	I would do?		you would be nicer to me.
	to do?		to speak to the manager.
What do you **want** from me?		I don't **want** anything from you.	
What was he **hoping** for?		He was **hoping** I would ask him out.	
What does she **want** you to do?		She **wants** me to work late.	
Where do you **wish** you could go?		I **wish** I could go to Europe.	

B. *Pair work* **Discuss the following with your partner.**

1. What are some things you want in life?
2. What's something you hope you can do one day?
3. Who do you wish you could meet?
4. What's something you wish someone would do?

Communication

A time for change

A. *Pair work* **Use the prompts below to ask and answer questions. Answer using *wish, hope, or want.***

B. *Group work* **Choose a problem card from the pile your teacher gives you. Read your card carefully. Put it back in the pile and explain the problem to your group in your own words. Each person in your group should give advice.**

You want your wife to quit her job. You think she should take care of the house and children. Your wife refuses because she would be bored.

I have a great relationship with my wife but she really loves her job. I hoped that she would stay home and look after the children. She says that if she gave up her job her life would be boring.

Have you thought about quitting your job and staying home?

Why don't you ask her to work part-time?

UNIT

6 New Products

Warm Up

Would you buy it?

A. ***Pair work*** **Discuss the following products in the pictures below. How useful are they?**

B. ***Pair work*** **Ask and answer the following questions with a partner.**

1. Which of the above products looks the most useful? Why do you think so?
2. What new products have you bought? Why did you buy them?
3. What are some new products that have come out recently? What do you think of them?
4. How do you decide if a product is worth buying or not?

Listening

TV commercials

T09

A. Listen and answer the following questions. Check your answers with a partner.

1. What type of product is being sold in each commercial? What are the products' names?
2. What does the woman in the first commercial say about her husband after he uses the product?
3. What does the product in the second commercial smell and taste like?
4. How does the third product sound to the person in the commercial?

B. *Pair work* Ask and answer the following questions with a partner.

1. Which commercial is the most interesting? Why do you think so?
2. What was the best / worst TV commercial you've seen? Why was it so good / bad?
3. How much do you rely on ads when you buy products? Explain.
4. Do you ever feel annoyed by commercials? When? Why?

Talk Tips

Idioms related to *likes* and *dislikes*

A. Read the following idioms related to likes and dislikes. What does each one mean?

I could **go for** that.
The last one I tried really **turned my stomach**.
I'm **not in the mood** for it.
It'll **grow on** you.

B. Match the expressions in bold on the left with their definitions on the right. Check your answers with a partner.

1. It **made my skin crawl**.
2. He could **care less** for what he thinks.
3. Taking that bus is **for the birds**.
4. They **sing praises** about her any time her name is mentioned.
5. He really **took a shine** to that new toy.
6. She just **loves** him **to bits**.

___ To not be interested in
___ To like or love someone a lot
___ To be foolish
___ To like something right away
___ To cause a negative emotional and physical reaction
___ To say a lot of good things about someone

C. *Pair work* Ask and answer the following questions with a partner.

1. When have you not been in the mood to do something, but your friends wanted you to?
2. Describe an experience that made your skin crawl. Why did you feel this way?
3. What is something that took time to grow on you until you eventually liked it?
4. Have you ever felt like you wanted to sing praises about someone? Why?

Language Focus
Verbs of sense

A. With a partner, ask and answer the questions below.

QUESTIONS			ANSWERS
How	do I does he/she does it	**look?**	You **look** great. He **looks** younger.
What		**look like?**	She **looks like** a model. It **looks like** a computer.
How	does it	**smell?** **taste?**	It **smells** good. It **tastes** disgusting.
What		**smell like?** **taste like?**	It **smells like** pizza. It **tastes like** chocolate.
How	does it	**sound?** **feel?**	It **sounds** wonderful. It **feels** smooth.
What		**sound like?** **feel like?**	It **sounds like** a crying baby. It **feels like** plastic.
What does your friend **look like?** Why don't you like your soup? What do you think of the food? Do you like this song?			She **looks** young. She **looks like** an actress. It **smells like** tomato soup, but it **tastes like** fish. The spaghetti **tastes** amazing. No, the singer **sounds like** a screaming cat.

B. *Pair work* **Discuss the following with your partner.**

1. Have you ever eaten something that looked delicious but tasted bad? Describe it.
2. What are some things that feel soft / hard / smooth / rough?
3. Who do you look like? How so?
4. What are some things you think smell good / bad?

Communication

What an amazing new product!

A. **Imagine a new kind of product (electronic device, appliance, car, food, item of clothing, etc.). Circle the verbs of your choice, and fill in the blanks below to describe what it is like.**

It looks/sounds/smells/tastes/feels *stylish*.
It looks/sounds/smells/tastes/feels ____________________.
It looks/sounds/smells/tastes/feels like ____________________.
It looks/sounds/smells/tastes/feels like ____________________.

B. ***Group work*** **Take turns asking questions to try and guess what your group members' products are.**

Does it look expensive?

Yes, it does. These kinds of things are usually expensive.

Does it taste sweet?

I'm sorry, but you don't eat this.

C. ***Class work*** **Your group will choose its favorite product from part B, and make a short TV commercial for it. When ready, groups will present their commercials to the class.**

Have you ever wished you didn't have to clean your house? That day has come! This looks like a computer mouse, but it's a new robot.

What a useful robot! Did you say it cooks like a professional chef? Did you say its deserts taste incredible?

UNIT

7 Urban Legends

Warm Up

Is it true, or a modern myth?

A. Which of the stories below are true and which are false? Check your answers with a partner.

Elvis lives! There have been many recent Elvis sightings. Did he really die in 1977? It's possible that the *King* still lives and ...

The Men in Black: These mysterious people are the agents of a great conspiracy.

21 people died in a flood of molasses in Boston, America.

The Apollo moon landing was a fake.

Fan death: Sleeping next to a fan at night can kill you.

B. *Pair work* Ask and answer the following questions with a partner.

1. Which story above is the most difficult to believe? Why?
2. Can you think of other urban legends or conspiracy theories that are not shown above?
3. Do you enjoy TV shows or movies that tell stories about conspiracy theories? Why / Why not?
4. Why do people continue to believe in conspiracy theories and urban legends?

Listening

It's a conspiracy! T10

A. Listen and answer the following questions. Check your answers with a partner.

1. What did the stranger say his friend had information about? What happened to his friend?
2. What did the man see last week? Where was this?
3. How was Elvis Presley involved?
4. What's Mike's opinion of this man? How can you tell?

B. *Pair work* Ask and answer the following questions with a partner.

1. What do you think about the stranger's story?
2. What do you think really happened to the man's friend?
3. What famous people from your country could have faked their deaths? Why would they have done so?
4. What would you do if someone approached you like the stranger in the story?

Pronunciation

Changes in consonant clusters

A. Listen and repeat. Notice the deleted consonant sounds. T11

My friend sent me a computer disk.	His landlady said that he had moved out.
They told me that I shouldn't make the same mistake.	Exactly! This is my stop!
He talked about a conspiracy.	I didn't want to listen to him!

B. *Pair work* Choose from the words above to make a statement or question, and start a short conversation with your partner. Practice pronouncing words with deleted consonants.

Exactly what did your friend say he saw?

He saw two men get out of a black car. They were dressed in black suits and wore dark sunglasses.

Language Focus
Reported speech

A. With a partner, ask and answer the questions below.

QUOTATIONS		
"I'm innocent!" -Man accused of murder	"You have to do your homework." -Your teacher	"What are you talking about?" -Your best friend
"I saw a UFO in my back yard." -UFO witness	"That's impossible." -You (in reaction to the above)	"Have you heard about the fire?" -A woman on the bus

QUESTIONS	ANSWERS
What did the guy on trial say? Did that guy confess?	He said that he was innocent. He claimed he was innocent.
What did that lady tell you? What did she say?	She told me she saw a UFO in her back yard. She claims to have seen a UFO.
What did the teacher tell you? What did he talk about?	He said I had to do my homework. He told me to do my homework.
What did you say? How did you react?	I told him it was impossible. I said that it was impossible.
What did your friend say? What did she ask you?	She asked me what I was talking about. She wondered what I was talking about.
What did that woman say? Did she ask you something?	She asked if I had heard about some fire. She asked me whether I had heard about the fire.

B. ***Pair work*** **Discuss the following with your partner.**

1. What did your teachers always tell you when you were in high school?
2. What has someone asked you recently? What did you tell them?
3. Has anyone ever told you something strange?
4. What would you ask your favorite actor/actress if you met them?

Communication

Have you heard about this?

A. **Your teacher will assign you one of the following topics. Create statements about your topic by writing in the blanks below.**

…› *Many people in Seoul said that they had seen Marilyn Monroe*.

…› ______________________________.

…› ______________________________.

…› ______________________________.

B. ***Group work*** **Your group will discuss and create a story about your topic from part A. Use your group's favorite sentences from part A, and create any extra information you want. Fill in the form on the right with key information about your story.**

Alligators live in the New York city sewers!

Basic Idea:

- *New Yorkers bought baby alligators and flushed them down toilets to get rid of them.*

Reported statements:

- *Some people suggested that the animals might have survived.*

____

Basic Idea:

-

Reported statements:

-

C. ***Class work*** **Your group will now present its imaginary story to the class. Use reported statements, and try hard to make it sound real.**

Our government captured alien spaceships, but they won't admit the truth.

It's true! Hundreds of people said that they had seen UFOs flying above one of our air-force bases.

UNIT

8 Prejudice

Warm Up

Snap judgments

A. Match the appearance/characteristics of the people in A to the typical beliefs about them in B. Compare your answers with a partner.

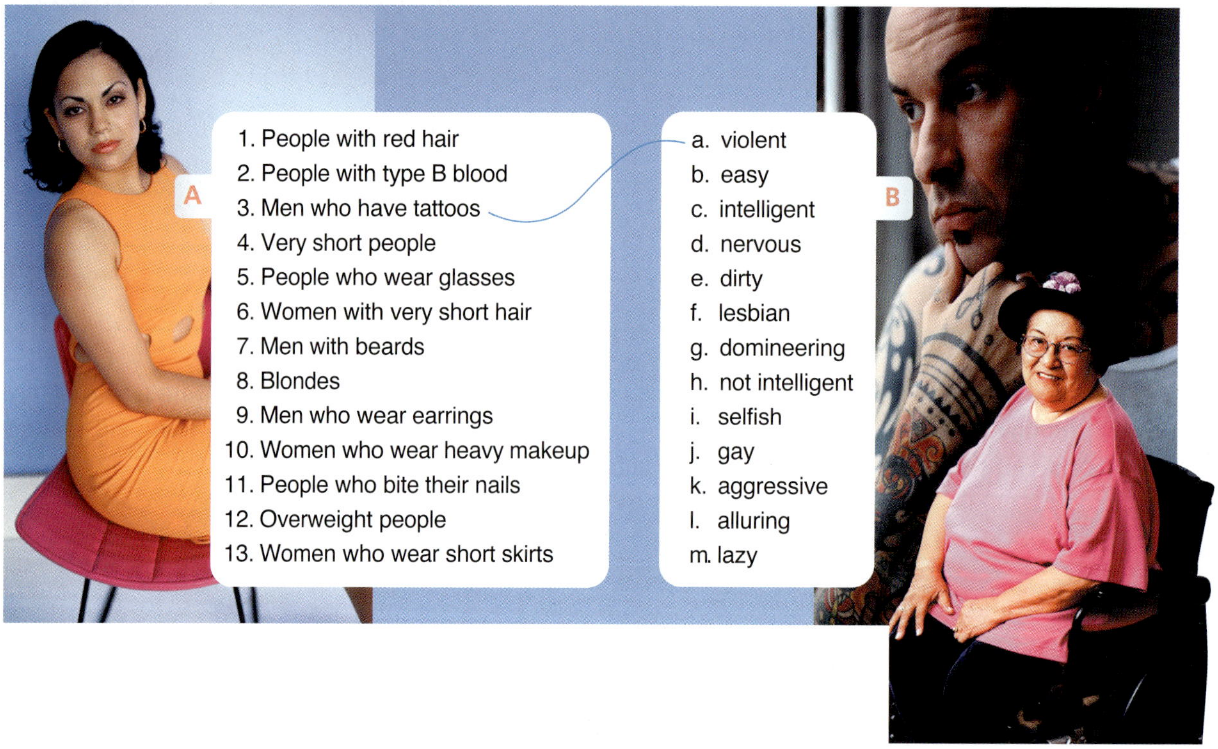

A

1. People with red hair
2. People with type B blood
3. Men who have tattoos
4. Very short people
5. People who wear glasses
6. Women with very short hair
7. Men with beards
8. Blondes
9. Men who wear earrings
10. Women who wear heavy makeup
11. People who bite their nails
12. Overweight people
13. Women who wear short skirts

B

a. violent
b. easy
c. intelligent
d. nervous
e. dirty
f. lesbian
g. domineering
h. not intelligent
i. selfish
j. gay
k. aggressive
l. alluring
m. lazy

B. ***Pair work*** **Ask and answer the following questions with a partner.**

1. Do you think any of the comments above are offensive/funny?
2. Do you believe most people make judgments like the ones in part A when they first meet someone?
3. Is it dangerous to make judgments like these? Why/Why not?
4. What kind of "snap judgments" do you think people might make about you?

Listening

They're all like that. T12

A. Listen and answer the following questions. Check your answers with a partner.

1. What do you think Bob meant when he said the man they were watching was "one of them"?
2. Was Bob correct? How do you know?
3. What does Jodi think about Bob's opinion of the man in the mall? How do you know?
4. What is it that Bob objects to about "them"?

B. *Pair work* Ask and answer the following questions with a partner.

1. Do you think Bob was prejudiced in any way?
2. What are most people's feelings toward the people Bob was talking about ?
3. Do you think "they" should be allowed to get married and adopt children?
4. Can you give examples of different ways in which people may be prejudiced?

Talk Tips

Idioms of confusion and mistake

A. Read the following expressions related to confusion and mistake. What does each one mean?

I think you're **way off**.	You're not **thinking straight**.
You **screwed up**, Bob!	I think we're talking **at crossed purposes**.

B. Match the idioms below to the situations. Give your own examples for each idiom based on your experiences.

You call your wife/husband by your ex-girlfriend's/boyfriend's name. ___

You ask a girl when she's expecting and she tells you she's not pregnant. ___

1. There's been a bit of a mix-up.
2. You made a slip of the tongue.
3. You put your foot in your mouth.
4. You got your wires crossed.

You ordered 24 boxes of 12″ discs. You received 12 boxes of 24″ discs. ___

You ask a girl/guy out for dinner. You thought it was a date, he/she thinks it's a business dinner. ___

Language Focus

all (of) / some (of) / most (of)

A. With a partner, ask and answer the questions below.

QUESTIONS		ANSWERS
What do you think about How do you feel about What's your opinion on What's your take on	politicians? lawyers? climate change? those people?	I think **all** politicians are corrupt. **All of** the lawyers in my city are great. **Some** people don't think it's real. It scares me. **Some of** them are nice. Not all of them are bad.
Tell me about	your friends. your classmates. your classes. your teammates.	**Most of** them are students. **A few of** them have jobs. **Many of** them live in the same dorm. **None of** my classes are fun. **Every one of** them is boring. **Some of** them are really good. **None of** them are bad.

FURTHER EXAMPLES	
All men are dogs. **Every** terrorist should be killed. **Most** people would agree with me. **Some** people just have no clue. **Few** people really understand what that means. **No** politician should have that much power.	**All of** my friends loved that movie. **Every one of** my students did their homework. **Most of** the people here are from China. **Some of** my coworkers are going out later. **Few of** my teammates care if we win or lose. **None of** my grandparents can come to the reunion.

B. *Pair work* **Discuss the following with your partner.**

1. What do you think is true about all people?
2. What do some of your friends like that you don't?
3. What do you think is true about most politicians / athletes / men / women?
4. What are some things that no human can do?

Communication

A few good men

A. ***Pair work*** **Give your opinions about each of the topics below using the target structure. Your partner should agree or disagree with your ideas.**

1. Teenagers

2. Politicians

3. Doctors

4. Pro athletes

5. Stay-at-home dads

6. Feminine men

None of the politicians in this country are honest.

That's not true. Most of them do a good job and do their best to improve the country.

B. ***Group work*** **How likely is it that the situations below will become common? Rate each picture on a scale of 1 (won't happen) to 5 (very probable). Compare your answers with your group members.**

Female construction worker

Female President of the United States

Men and women competing against each other in the Olympics

Do you think men will ever have babies?

No, I don't think that will ever happen. None of the men I know would ever want to become pregnant.

UNIT

9 In The News

Warm Up

Keeping up with the news

A. **Rate the different kinds of news below from 1 (the most interesting) to 6 (the least interesting). Compare your answers with a partner.**

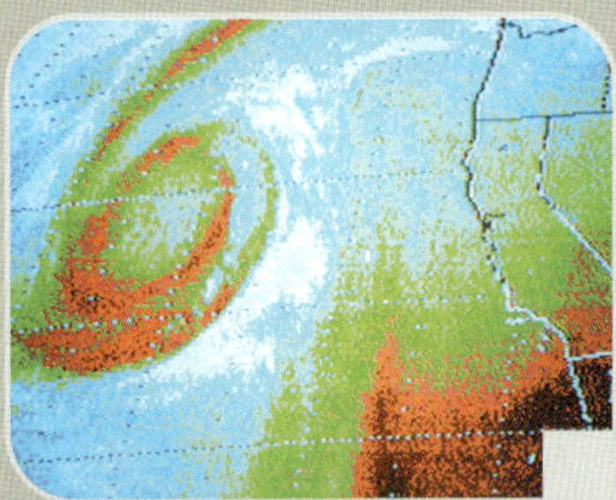

Weather News

Sports News

World News

Entertainment News

Local News

Financial News

I like the financial news best because my major is economics.

Really? I hate it but I love sports news best.

B. ***Pair work*** **Ask and answer the following questions with a partner.**

1. When do you like to watch, listen to, or read about the news?
2. Do you prefer to find out about the news from TV, radio, newspaper, or online? Why?
3. In your opinion, what is the best TV news program or newspaper in your country?
4. Do you ever get news information from foreign sources? Which ones? How often?
5. Do you ever feel that there are some news sources that you can't trust? Why?

Listening

A young star goes to court. T13

A. Listen and answer the following questions. Check your answers with a partner.

1. What was Johnny Liebling accused of doing? What was some of the evidence?
2. Why had he been having trouble recently?
3. What did Johnny Liebling say about what happened?
4. What was the result of the trial? Were there any penalties?

B. *Pair work* Ask and answer the following questions with a partner.

1. What do you think of the jury's decisions about the actor? Explain.
2. Do you think the punishment would have been worse if the actor wasn't rich and famous? Why?
3. Do you think the actor will continue to be successful, Why / Why not?
4. What advice would you give the actor if you were his friend / coworker?

Talk Tips

Idioms of self-control

A. Read the following idioms of self-control. What does each one mean?

He was having trouble **keeping his cool**.	He was **getting carried away**.
He needed to **get his act together**.	He seemed more **levelheaded**.

B. Match the expressions on the left with their definitions on the right. Check your answers with a partner.

1. Get a hold of yourself!
2. She always keeps her wits about her.
3. Don't lose your head!
4. You'd better keep on your toes.
5. Hold it!

___ Be careful.
___ Don't get excited/lose control!
___ Regain your self-control!
___ She is always in control.
___ Don't express your anger!

C. *Pair work* Ask and answer the following questions with a partner.

1. Have you ever known someone who needed to get their act together? What happened?
2. What jobs really need people who can keep their cool? Why?
3. Can you remember a time when you lost your head over something? Explain.
4. When you are upset, what do you do to try to get a hold of yourself?

Language Focus

Passive voice

A. **With a partner, ask and answer the questions below.**

QUESTIONS	ANSWERS
What happened? What happened here? What happened to your car? What happened to the window?	He **was hit** by a car. The table **was knocked** over. My car **was stolen**. It **was broken** some time last night.
What's happening? What's going on?	That guy **is being arrested**. She's **being punished** for hitting the other girl. The computer **is being fixed**. A movie **is being made** here.
What are the rules? Are there any restrictions? What are the requirements? Are there any special procedures?	People **aren't allowed** into the courtroom. You're not **allowed** to take pictures. A report must **be filed**. All visitors must **be signed** in.
Where's Bob? What's going on with the copy machine? Did you get your car fixed? How old is that building?	He **was taken to the hospital.** It's **being replaced**. It's **being fixed** as we speak. It **was built** in the 1920s.

B. ***Group work*** **Look at the pictures below and imagine news stories that explain each one. Discuss what you think happened.**

Communication

The evening news

A. You will be given a news topic. Imagine what happened and write details about it.

- *For:* General news
  - Lead story
- *Story:* (Name)
  - Downtown disaster!
- *Details:*
  - Many people were injured.
  - Buildings were damaged.

- *For:*
- *Story:*
- *Details:*

B. *Group work* Your group will plan and practice a TV news broadcast. Be prepared to present your work in part C.

Start TV anchorman/woman: lead story

Finish TV anchorman/woman: last comments

What should we have after the lead story and general news?

How about sports news? I could talk about a soccer game. Let's say ...

C. *Class work* Your group will now role-play its news broadcast. When it's not your group's turn, listen carefully to the other groups' presentations and be ready to respond with comments or questions.

UNIT 10 Helping Out

Warm Up
Ways people volunteer

A. **Read about different ways in which people volunteer in the UK. Fill in the pie chart to show how you think people in your country volunteer. Compare your answers with a partner.**

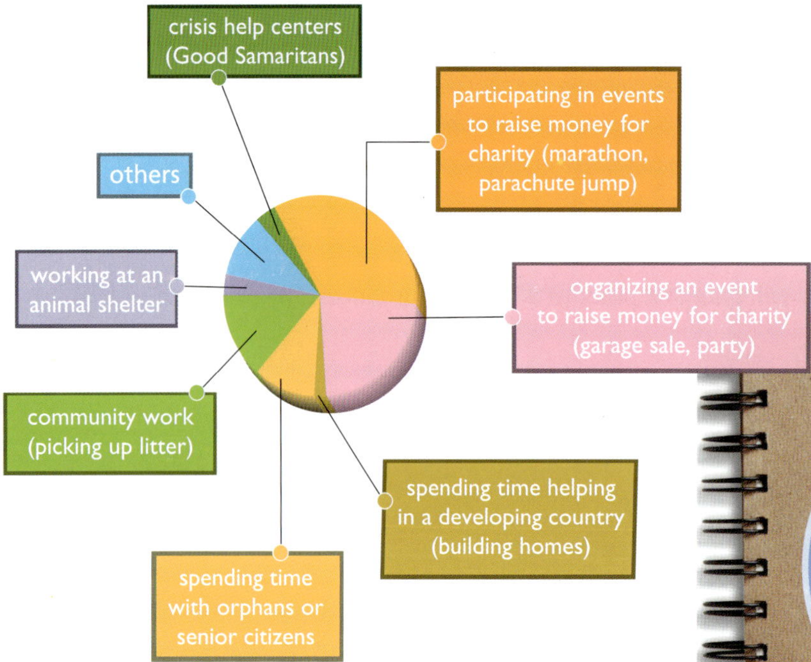

B. *Pair work* **Ask and answer the following questions with a partner.**

1. Is volunteering popular in your country?
2. Is there a big difference in the way people volunteer in your country and in the UK?
3. Have you ever volunteered for any of the things above?
4. Do you plan to do any of the activities in the future? Which ones?
5. Would you be willing to spend one year helping others in a developing country?
6. Can you think of other ways in which people volunteer?

Listening

Your country needs you.

A. Listen and answer the following questions. Check your answers with a partner.

1. What do a lot of people think about Raynor's method of raising money?
2. Describe how Raynor's event raises money for charity.
3. In your own words, describe how Raynor was feeling before the jump.
4. Why does Clive volunteer?
5. What volunteer work does he do?

B. ***Pair work*** **Ask and answer the following questions with a partner.**

1. Would you do a parachute jump if you could raise a lot of money for charity?
2. Would you be willing to do any of the following things for charity: run a marathon, bungee jump, a car wash, a long walk, shave your head?
3. Do you know of any places similar to where Clive volunteered? Would you enjoy working in a place like that?
4. What kind of volunteer work would you be most likely to do: environmental, educational, community, or political?

Pronunciation

Syllable stress

A. Listen and repeat. Notice the stressed syllables.

prepa**ra**tion	do**na**tion	tra**di**tion	compli**ca**tion

B. Show where the stress is located in the following words then compare your ideas with a partner.

contribution	satisfaction	organization	assassination
musician	electrician	explosion	compassion

Language Focus
Non-referential *it* and *there*

A. With a partner, ask and answer the questions below.

QUESTIONS			ANSWERS
Is **it** Would **it** be	OK a good idea bad	to help them? to give cash? to quit?	**It** would be nice of you to help them. **It**'s safer to use a credit card. **It**'s never good to quit.
What do you think about	that? volunteering? working overtime?		**It**'s a shame that some people abuse animals. **It**'s a wonderful thing to volunteer. **It**'s too hard to work so late.
How long does **it** take to How long will **it** take to	find a new owner? get there? make a difference? find a new job?		**It** usually takes a few weeks to find one. **It** will take about an hour to get there. **It** doesn't take long to make a difference. **It**'ll take forever to find a new job.
Why do you volunteer? What did you see? How many people are coming? Should I do it?			**There**'s a tradition in my family of volunteering. **There** were a lot of abandoned dogs in the streets. **There** will be 20 of us all together. **There**'s nothing wrong with it.
What do you need? What can I do for you? Is **there** something I can help you with? Is **there** anything else?			**There**'s something I have to ask you. **There** are a few problems we need to talk about. **There** are a couple of questions I'd like to ask you. **There**'s always something else to do.

B. *Pair work* **Discuss the following with your partner.**

1. What would happen if everyone had to give money to charity each month?
2. Why don't more people volunteer?
3. Why are there homeless people on the streets of a modern city?
4. Why can't the government give more assistance to the poor?

Communication

What kind of volunteer are you?

A. *Pair work* **You work for an organization that places volunteers into the project that is most suitable for them. First, ask and answer the questions from the survey with your partner.**

Volunteer Information Form

Personal information

*Name: *Age: *Job/School: *Male ☐ Female ☐

SURVEY

QUESTIONS	ANSWERS
1. What kinds of things are you interested in at the moment?	
2. Is there a job that you would really like to do in the future?	
3. Are you interested in any political party?	
4. Do you have your own transportation?	
5. Can you cook?	
6. Do you have any friends that would like to volunteer with you?	
7. How would your partner or parents feel about your volunteering?	
8. Do you enjoy working alone or as part of a team?	
9. Are you a good listener?	
10. Would you be willing to use all of your summer holidays to volunteer?	
11. Do you enjoy organizing things?	
12. Would you be willing to take six months off work to volunteer?	
13. Would you be willing to travel abroad as a volunteer?	

14. Would you be prepared to volunteer in the following situations?
earthquake relief ☐ famine relief ☐ war relief ☐ tsunami relief ☐

15. Do you have skill in any of the following areas?
computer ☐ artistic/music ☐ language ☐
engineering ☐ construction ☐ health care ☐

16. Which of the following best describes you?
shy ☐ patient ☐ dependable ☐ determined ☐ confident ☐ sociable ☐

17. Which of the following do you see yourself as?
I just go along with everyone else. ☐ I have to be in charge. ☐ It depends — I can do both. ☐

18. Would you object to working with any of the following groups?
young children ☐ teenagers ☐ seniors ☐ physically handicapped ☐
mentally handicapped ☐ homeless people ☐ drug addicts ☐ alcoholics ☐

19. How much free time do you have?
as much as I want ☐ my weekends are free ☐
a few hours a week ☐ almost none ☐

B. *Group work* **Form groups and decide what kind of volunteer work would be most suitable for each person. Give reasons for your choices.**

C. *Class work* **Choose one of the surveys to present to the class. The speaker should not say who they are talking about. Can you guess who it is? Do you agree with the volunteer work they have been assigned?**

Communication Helpers

Making recommendations

There are several reasons why you should/shouldn't ...
There are opportunities for you to get involved with ...
There is an organization I know that ...
There is nothing you ...
It is obvious that you should ...
It's important for you to get involved with ...
It might be a good idea for you to ...
It isn't a good idea for you to ...

UNIT

11 Friendship

Warm Up

What is a friend?

A. *Class work* **What should friends have in common? Add words in the empty boxes.**

B. *Pair work* **Place checks (✓) in the table below, then discuss your ideas and opinions with a partner.**

	VERY IMPORTANT	IMPORTANT	NEUTRAL	NOT IMPORTANT
language	✓			
money				

What is important in having a successful friendship?

Well, I think it's very important that friends speak the same language because they can communicate easily.

C. *Pair work* **Ask and answer the following questions with a partner.**

1. Have you ever had a best friend of the opposite sex?
2. What is the biggest age gap you know of between friends?
3. Do friendships change when one friend gets married?
4. Is it possible for a divorced couple to remain friends?
5. Do you have/Have you had any foreign friends?

Listening

Friends are like diamonds. T 16

A. Listen and answer the following questions. Check your answers with a partner.

1. Who is Ramsay? Is he a person? How do you know?
2. In the second passage, what kinds of things have Alison and the speaker done together?
3. In the third passage, how did the speaker meet Yuki?
4. What do Yuki and the speaker have in common?

B. *Pair work* Ask and answer the following questions with a partner.

1. Is it possible to be friends with your parents?
2. Do friends become more or less important to you as you get older? Why?
3. Are there any friendships you have to work hard at keeping?
4. How do you know when a friend is not a true friend?

Talk Tips

Proverbs related to friendship

A. Read the following proverbs related to friendship.

A friend in need is a friend indeed.	A problem shared is a problem halved.
A friend to everybody is a friend to nobody.	A good friend is sooner lost than won.

B. *Pair work* Match the proverbs above with the definitions below.

1. Telling your friend about a difficulty will make the difficulty easier to endure.
2. A person that gives you help when you truly need it is a true friend.
3. It is difficult to keep friends but easy to lose them.
4. A person who tries to be friends with all people cannot be a committed friend as well.

C. *Class work* Make a short dialogue relating to one of the proverbs above and practice it with a partner. Then present it to your class members and see if they can guess the proverb.

A: I'm so stressed out these days.
B: What's wrong?
A: You don't want to hear about it. It's really boring and depressing.
B: Hey, I'm your friend. Maybe you'll feel better if you tell me.

Language Focus

Phrasal verbs with *break*, *call* and *do*

A. With a partner, ask and answer the questions below.

QUESTIONS		ANSWERS
What happened to What's going on with	your girlfriend? your wedding plans? your car? your apartment?	She **broke up** with me. It's not happening. We **broke off** the engagement. It **broke down** again. I had to walk to work. Somebody **broke in** and stole my TV.
Have you talked to Jan lately? Are we still going to the game tonight? Have you seen your grandmother recently? Why wasn't Bill at work today?		No, I haven't. Let's **call** her **up**. No, it's been **called off**. I **call on** her about once a week. He **called in** this morning.
Are you hungry? What are you going to do to your house? What will you do if he quits? Why are you so tired?		Yeah, I could **do with** some food. We're going to **do up** the living room and bathroom. Nothing. We can **do without** him. The basketball game really **did** me **in**.

B. ***Pair work*** **Discuss the following with your partner.**

1. Who have you broken up with? Who has broken up with you?
2. Have you ever been disappointed because something was called off? What was it?
3. What could you do with right now?
4. What's something you couldn't do without?
5. What always does you in?

Communication

What kind of friend are you?

A. What makes a good friend and a bad friend? Write your ideas below, then share them with a partner.

Good friend

is always there for you

____

____

____

Bad friend

only thinks about themselves

____

____

____

B. *Pair work* You are going to make a questionnaire to find out if your classmates are good or bad friends. Think of three questions and write multiple choice answers for each question. Then write some comments for the "Results" section.

Example

Question: Someone starts telling you a rumor about your best friend. What do you do?

(a) Tell the person that it's impolite and unkind to spread rumors.
(b) Call your friend and ask if the rumor is true.
(c) Listen to the rumor, then discuss it with someone else.

Question 1

(a)

(b)

(c)

Question 2

(a)

(b)

(c)

Question 3

(a)

(b)

(c)

C. *Pair work* Your teacher will give you a piece of paper to write your questions and results on. Give each other the results.

D. *Group work* Ask and answer the following questions with your group.

1. Do you agree or disagree with the quiz results?
2. Have you actually been in any of the situations mentioned in the quiz questions?
3. What is the biggest sacrifice you would make for a friend?
4. What could you do to be a better friend?

UNIT

12 Lookism

Warm Up

Beauties from all across the globe

A. Match these representative beauties with the countries and cultures they're from. Compare your answers with a partner.

5

1. U.S.A.
2. Iran
3. France
4. China
5. Spain
6. Masai tribe

B. *Pair work* Choose your top two beauties and compare your answers with a partner. What do you think the pictures tell us about different cultures' ideals of beauty?

I chose the blond — I think it's Marilyn Monroe. I like blonds.

I do too, but I chose ...

C. *Pair work* Ask and answer the following questions with a partner.

1. In your country, has the concept of the ideal beauty changed over time? How?
2. Do any of the people above have a "mysterious" beauty to them? Why / Why not?
3. Which person (living or dead) would you like to resemble if you could? Why?
4. Are there any types of appearance you don't find attractive? Give details.
5. Do you think beautiful people have better lives? Why / Why not?

Listening

Taking a look at "lookism" T17

A. Listen and answer the following questions. Check your answers with a partner.

1. What kind of place in Shooters?
2. What is Carl's problem with Shooters? How much is he suing them for?
3. Who is Byker Hoffman?
4. What did she find out about a clothing store chain?

B. *Pair work* Ask and answer the following questions with a partner.

1. Is Carl's complaint reasonable? Why / Why not?
2. What theme restaurants do you know of? What do the servers look like?
3. Do you think appearance-based hiring is common where you live? Explain.
4. Would you ever work at a place like the ones in the listening? Why / Why not?
5. Is "lookism" a hot topic where you live? Give details.

Talk Tips

Proverbs related to beauty and appearance

A. Read the following proverbs related to beauty and apperance. What does each one mean?

Beauty is only skin deep.	True beauty comes from within.
Beauty comes in all sizes.	Beauty is in the eye of the beholder.

B. Match the two parts of the proverbs by drawing a line between them. Check your answers with a partner.

All that glitters	can be deceiving.
You can't judge a book	is not gold.
Looks	by its cover.
Beauty is	as beauty does.

C. *Pair work* Ask and answer the following questions with a partner.

1. Which pairs or groups of proverbs are most similar in meaning?
2. In which situations might you use some of these proverbs? Describe.
3. Do you have any similar proverbs in your first language? What are they?
4. Which of the above proverbs do you like the best? Why?
5. Why don't more people follow the advice of these proverbs? Give details.

Language Focus

Stative verbs of cognition

A. With a partner, ask and answer the questions below.

QUESTIONS		ANSWERS
What do you **think** about	this class? her? that book? his opinion?	I **think** it's the best class I've ever taken. I **believe** she's the best player on the team. I **consider** it the worst book I've read this year. I **understand** his viewpoint, but I disagree.
Does he **consider** himself an educated man? Why do you **like** her so much? How do you **think** you'll do on the test? Why did you finally **ask** her out?		He **considers** himself the smartest person here. She **appreciates** good music and fine wine. I **doubt** I'll pass. I didn't study very much. I **noticed** she was looking at me a lot.
Do you **realize** how lucky you are? Do you **understand** what has to be done? Do you **regret** doing that? Do you **appreciate** all the help they've given you?		Yes, I **know** I've been fortunate. I **know** what I have to do. I don't **regret** it one bit. I **realize** I owe them a lot.
Are you optimistic about the future? What are your thoughts on the future?		I **believe** I will succeed. I **think** I'll be OK. I **doubt** I'll have any problems. I don't **think** it'll be easy, but I know I'll make it.

B. *Pair work* **Discuss the following with your partner.**

1. What's something you really appreciate? Why do you appreciate it?
2. Do you consider yourself a good person? What else do you consider yourself to be?
3. What's something you strongly believe? Why do believe that?
4. What's something you doubt will happen? Why do you doubt it?

Communication

Who looks good for the job?

A. *Pair work* **Look at the pictures and interviewer's notes below. Then choose only one of the job openings to fill and the two final candidates.**

Flashy Paradise, a cutting-edge fashion company known worldwide, has the following job openings:

Business negotiator
Overseas sales representative
Advertising/PR expert
Trainer
Product demonstrator/promoter
Import/Export specialist
Accountant
Product manager
Office manager

Todd

- *extremely well-dressed and prepared*
- *very charming, funny, well-spoken, and sincere*
- *seems just a bit shy (not too aggressive!)*
- *great background in law and politics*
- *Stanford graduate, knows three languages, 150+ IQ*

Ruth

- *old-fashioned dresser, but she realizes our company is "about brains and clothes"*
- *positive, but tough and aggressive*
- *well-traveled with a background in editing, writing, and negotiations*

Sam

- *well-dressed, well-prepared*
- *bright, well-spoken, and energetic (seems to be a perfectionist, but not sure??)*
- *Yale graduate, very athletic*
- *good management background*

Larry

- *formal dresser*
- *very outgoing, energetic, and postive (seems a bit proud, but not sure??)*
- *Stanford graduate, has M.B.A.*
- *considers himself an "expert" in law*

Lisa

- *very sharp dresser!*
- *talkative, lively, and positive, but seems a little bit emotional*
- *describes herself as "hot-tempered"*
- *has worked abroad, has PR background*

Both Todd and Ruth seem good for the negotiator job.

Yeah, tough choice. How about ...

B. *Group work* **Join another pair and compare the positions and finalists you chose. Together hire one person for one position.**

C. *Class work* **Who got hired? Take turns telling the other groups who you chose and why.**

Unit 1

so, too, either, neither

- Use ***so*** and ***too*** to agree with affirmative/positive statements.

  "I have one daughter." — "I do, ***too****."*

  "I'm exhausted." — "Me, ***too****."*

  *"I like curry." — "****So*** *do I."*

  *"I'm a freshman." — "****So*** *am I."*

- Use ***neither*** and ***not*** + ***either*** to agree with negative statements.

  *"I don't like Olga." — "I do****n't, either****."*

  "I'm not a music major." — "Me, ***neither****."*

  *"I've never been to Australia." — "****Neither*** *have I."*

  *"I can't concentrate because of the noise." — "****Neither*** *can I."*

- Notice the reverse word order in additive statements starting with ***so/neither***.

  "I'm a freshman." — "So ***am I****."* (NOT ~~*So I am.*~~)

  "I don't like curry." — "Neither ***do I****."*(NOT ~~*Neither I do.*~~)

- When ***So/Neither*** + **verb** + **subject** is used to mean "also"/"also not," always use an auxiliary, a modal, or form of ***be*** or ***do***.

  "I am hungry." — "So ***am*** *I."*

  "I don't play golf." — "Neither ***do*** *I."*

  "I haven't been to New York." — "Neither ***have*** *I."*

  "I can speak two languages." — "So ***can*** *I."*

Unit 2

Present perfect continuous

- Use the present perfect continuous to talk about actions that began in the past and continue to the present.

  *I **have been playing** in a band for five years.*

- **Form:** ***have/has + been + -ing***

I	**have**	**been**	**working**	very hard.
Lara	**has**	**been**	**studying**	web page design.

- ***For*** is used with the present perfect continuous when we wish to indicate how long something has been happening.

  *"How long **have** you **been working** here?"*

  *– "**I've been working** for this company **for** 10 years."*

- With negative statements, ***for*** can be replaced with ***in***.

  *We haven't seen her **in** ten years.*

- ***Since*** is used to indicate the point in time when the action/event began.

  *She**'s been living** in this house **since** 2000.*

- Sometimes the actions have been completed.

  *I'm exhausted because **I've been running**.*

  *I have no money now because **I've been shopping** all day.*

- Stative verbs (e.g. *like, love, know, be, have,* etc.) are not used in continuous forms. Use the present perfect instead.

  *I**'ve known** him for a few months.* (NOT I~~'ve been knowing~~ ...)

  *We**'ve had** this car for 6 years.* (NOT ~~We've been having~~ ...)

Unit 3

used to vs. *be/get used to*

1. *used to*

- Use ***used to*** + the base form of the verb to talk about past habits or states that don't occur now.
  *She **used to smoke**, but she quit last year.*
  *I **used to hate** big dogs, but now I have a St. Bernard.*

- Notice the spelling change in questions and negative statements.
  ***Did** you **use to** be afraid of ghosts?*
  *Omar **didn't use to** have that mustache.*

- Don't use ***used to*** for things that didn't happen regularly.
  *I ~~**used to eat**~~ camel meat a few times in Egypt.* (×)

2. *be/get used to*

- Use ***be used to*** **+ noun/gerund** to say that something is now familiar or acceptable.
  ***Are** you **used to** your new work schedule?*
  *I **am used to** getting up at 5 a.m.*

- Use ***get used to*** for emphasizing the process of change.
  *I'm slowly **getting used to** living in a big city.*

Unit 4

Gerunds as subjects and objects

- A **gerund** is a verb used as a noun. They are usually formed by adding *-ing* to a root verb, but in some cases the change involves some spelling differences:

  1. One syllable ending in a consonant, double the consonant (*hit* → *hi**tting***)
  2. Consonant and ***e*** ending, drop the ***e*** and add *-ing* (*smoke* → *smok**ing***)

- Most often gerunds are used to talk about actions in a general way, without expressing the time it takes place.

  *I enjoy **sailing**.*

  ***Singing** is something I'd rather avoid doing in public.*

- As a noun gerunds can take many positions in a sentence.

  1. Gerunds can be subjects of sentences.
     Notice the 3rd person singular verb form.
     ***Running marathons** requires mental and physical stamina.*
     *Does **watching TV** make people dumber?*
  2. Gerunds can serve as complements to the subject of a sentence.
     *My students' favorite activity is **sleeping**.*
  3. Gerunds are also used as objects. Notice the determiner before the gerund in the first sentence.
     *My wife doesn't like my **hanging out** late with coworkers.*
     *Seth enjoys **biking** on weekends.*
  4. Gerunds are often used as the object of a preposition.
     *I'm bored from **sitting** in meetings all day.*

Unit 5

want, hope, wish + infinitive or *that*-clause

- ***Want, hope,*** and ***wish*** can all be used to express the desire that a situation/event will happen in the future.

1. *want*

   - ***Want*** + **infinitive** is used for situations/events that could happen.
     *I **want to study** abroad next year.*
   - ***Want*** can also be followed by an object and complement.
     *The couple **wants** me to find their dog.*
     *We **want** it completed by Tuesday.*
   - ***Want*** cannot be followed by a ***that*-clause**.
     *I **wanted** you to spend more time with me.*
     (NOT ~~*I wanted that you spent more time with me.*~~)

2. *hope*

   - Use ***hope*** + **infinitive** or ***that*-clause** to talk about a future possibility.
     *Irene **hopes to be** a better person. She's working at it.*
     *I **hope** (that) you're coming to the party tonight.*
   - Notice how ***hope*** can be followed by *for*.
     *Let's **hope** for nice weather during our hike.*
   - ***Hope*** can be used in the present continuous form, but ***want*** and ***wish*** cannot.
     *Denise **is hoping** to get a new car.*
     He is ~~wanting/wishing~~ to swim.

3. *wish*

   - Use ***wish*** + **infinitive** to mean "want" with likely or unlikely events/situations
     *Dario **wishes to live** near the ocean.*
   - Use ***wish*** + ***that*-clause** to talk about future wishes that seem unlikely to come true.
     *I **wish** (that) I would win the lottery.* (It's not likely.)
   - Notice how ***wish*** is used to express regret and frustration.
     *I **wish** (that) you were more patient.* (but you are not)
     *I **wish** (that) you wouldn't be rude.* (but you are)

Unit 6

look + adjective vs. *look like* + noun

- ***Look***, ***sound***, ***taste***, ***smell***, and ***feel*** are stative verbs describing the senses.
- Use adjectives after these verbs when you want to express a quality.

subject	verb	adjective
That car	**looks**	**stylish**, doesn't it?
A teaching robot	**sounds**	**strange**, but it isn't.
The coffee	**tastes**	**bitter** this morning.
The kitchen	**smells**	**delicious**!
The new blanket	**feels**	**soft**.

- Use ***like*** + **noun phrase** after stative verbs of sense when you want to make a comparison (a simile).

subject	verb + *like*	noun
Andre	**looks like**	**a movie star**.
This bullet train	**sounds like**	**a jet**, doesn't it?
This new drink	**tastes like**	**milk**.
That alley	**smells like**	**garbage**.
The cloth	**feels like**	**silk**.

Note: Do not use stative verbs of sense in the continuous form unless you want to emphasize change.

*The beer's **tasting** much better now.*

*I'm **feeling** much better.*

Unit 7

Reported speech

- When reporting someone else's speech, use **reporting structures** made up of a **reporting clause** + **reported clause**.
- Most reported clauses begin with ***that*** or an **infinitive**:

reporting clause	reported clause
containing the reporting verb	containing reported information
*I **told** him* *She **said***	***to go** home.* ***that** they weren't home.*

- Most reported clauses begin with ***that*** or an **infinitive**. In reported speech, ***that*** serves as a conjunction and can be dropped.
  *She said **(that)** she didn't care.*
  *The doctor told him **to drink** plenty of liquid.*
- Notice how the person and verb tense changes in reported speech.

  1. Simple present → Simple past
     *Al said "**I don't know.**" → Al said (that) **he didn't know**.*
  2. Simple past → Past perfect
     *"**I moved**," Liz said. → Liz said (that) **she had moved**.*
  3. Present perfect → Past perfect
     *"**You've lost** weight," Kim said.*
     *→ Kim told **me** (that) **I had lost** weight.*

- Verbs in direct speech which take a past perfect or past perfect continuous form do not change.
  *"I **had packed** everything before the movers came," Daniel said.*
  *→ Daniel said he **had packed** everything before the movers came.*

  *"I **had been running** for three years before I tried a marathon," said Curtis.*
  *→ Curtis said he **had been running** for three years before he tried a marathon.*
- There is no tense change with present tense reporting verbs (e.g. *says*).
  *Mr. Bell: "The meeting **will be** delayed."*
  *→ Mr. Bell says the meeting **will be** delayed.*
- Use the same tense if you're reporting on something that is still true.
  *"I like baseball." → I told him I **like** baseball.*

Unit 8

all, some, most, many, a few, no(ne) (+of)

- Use **quantifiers** to refer to an indefinite number of people / things when making general statements.

  Every *teacher I know comes from outside Korea.*

  Most *new companies fail in the first year.*

  A few *couples want to adopt children from Cambodia.*

  No *Americans I know believe that!*

- Use ***a few*** and ***many*** with count nouns.

  a few *pencils* ***many*** *cars*

- Use ***a little*** and ***much*** with non-count nouns.

  a little *water* ***much*** *money*

- Use these quantifiers with both count and non-count nouns:

	Count nouns	Non-count
all	***all*** *men*	***all*** *literature*
most	***most*** *people*	***most*** *furniture*
some	***some*** *oranges*	***some*** *bread*
any	*(not)* ***any*** *friends*	*(not)* ***any*** *money*
no	***no*** *friends*	***no*** *hope*

- Quantifiers can be followed by ***of*** phrases to show parts of a specific group. Notice the articles and determiners.

  All of *us have college degrees, but* ***many of*** *us are unemployed.*

  Most of *the people I know love smooth jazz.*

  Some of *the kids in my class have pet spiders.*

  A few of *my friends like him.*

  None of *the guys I've met like romantic comedies.*

- Use only the quantifier when you talk about groups in general.

  Most *Koreans eat special foods on holidays. (~~Most of Koreans~~ ...)*

Unit 9

Passive voice

- **Form:** ***be*** **+ the past participle**

- The object in an active sentence becomes the subject of a passive sentence.
  *The police caught **the thieves**.* (active)
  ***The thieves** were caught by the police.* (passive)

- You can use ***by*** + **noun** to show who or what performs an action.
  *Harry Potter was written **by J.K. Rowling**.*

- Use the passive:
  1. when the agent (the "doer") is unknown, unimportant, or obvious.
     My bag was stolen yesterday. (I don't know who stole it.)
  2. when the main topic of the sentence is not the agent.
     The company was founded in 1881. (The founder is unimportant.)
  3. in formal reports, news articles, etc.
     More than 2000 people were killed by the earthquake.

- **Simple present passive**

Subject + ***am/are/is*** + **past participle**
*I **am needed** by my family.* *Both men **are wanted** by the police.*

- **Simple past passive**

Subject + ***was/were*** + **past participle**
*They **were punished** by the judge.* *That law **was made** in 2005.*

Unit 10

Non-referential *it* & *there*

1. Non-referential *it*

- Use non-referential ***it*** as a subject for **time**, **weather**, **distance**, and **environment**.

  It*'s March 14th.* ***It*** *hasn't rained for a while.*

  How far is ***it*** *from Chicago to Detroit?*

  It *gets a little noisy after classes let out.*

- There is another non-referential *it* which we want to call **preparatory *it***. The thing ***it*** refers to is within the sentence.

  It*'s great* ***to volunteer for things****.*

  I find ***it*** *rewarding* ***to work at an animal shelter****.*

2. Non-referential *there*

- Non-referential ***there*** serves as a subject, most often followed by *be*:

  There are *many books on the table.*

  There were *several animal attacks last month.*

- A few other verbs can be used after ***there***.

  There have been *many volunteers who joined us.*

  There came *three strange men on the street.*

Unit 11

Phrasal verbs with *break, call, do*

- Phrasal verbs consist of a verb and one or two **particles.**
  Transitive phrasal verbs take direct objects.
  Sometimes noun phrases can go either between the verb and particle or after the particle.
  ***Take off** your shoes.* ***Take** your shoes **off**.*
- Other transitive phrasal verbs can't be separated.
  Nouns must come after the particle.
  *We can't **do without** true friends.*
  (NOT ~~*do true friends without*~~)
  *Honey, I could **do with** some help cleaning.*
  (NOT ~~*do some help with*~~)
- With separable verbs, pronouns always go between the verb and the particle.
  *Why don't you **call** her **up**?* (NOT ~~*call up her*~~)
- Intransitive phrasal verbs do not take any direct objects and cannot be separated.
  *I usually **get up** early.*
- ***Do up*** can be separated.
  *Let's **do up** the bathrooms. Let's **do** the bathrooms **up**.*
- ***Call off*** is separable while ***call on*** isn't.
  *We were sorry to hear that you **called** your wedding **off**.*
  *But please **call on** us* (NOT ~~*call us on*~~) *the next time you need cake.*
- ***Break down*** and ***break up (with)*** can't be separated.
  Break off is separable, but often isn't separated in speech.
  *We **broke off** our engagement after our van **broke down**.*

Unit 12

Stative verbs of cognition (e.g. *think, doubt)*

- Use stative verbs to describe states or conditions that will not change, or is unlikely to change.
- Stative verbs can be classified into 5 categories:

possession	*have, belong to, owns, include, possess*
perception	*hear, see, taste, smell, look, appear*
emotion	*like, feel, love, need, wish, envy, adore*
relation	*contain, weigh, consist of, deserve, be*
cognition	*seem, believe, know, forget, think, realize, appreciate, understand, regret*

- Stative verbs of cognition describe activities related to thinking:

  *I **think** beauty is important in choosing a mate.*

  *Renee's argument **seems** logical, doesn't it?*

  *Dudley **appreciates** good looks and trendy fashions.*

- Stative verbs are not usually used in the continuous form.

  *I have **known** you for three years.* (NOT ~~*I have been knowing*~~)

Unit 1

Listening Track 02

Craig meets Ben, an old friend he hasn't seen for a long time, at a party.

B = Ben C = Craig L = Lucy

B : Craig? Is that you?

C : I'm sorry, have we met before?

B : It's Ben, Ben Willis. We went to elementary school together.

C : Oh, yeah, Ben. Wow, it's been a while. What are you up to these days?

B : Not too much. I just got back from Egypt. I have to find a job now.

C : Yeah, me too. It's hard, isn't it? There's not much out there at the moment, but I have a few interviews lined up next week.

B : I do, too. Let's keep our fingers crossed ... I'm glad to see you though, Craig. I don't know anyone at this party.

C : No, I don't, either, but things are looking up. A girl from one of my classes just walked in. Come on, I'll introduce you.

B : Oh, I don't know, Craig. I won't know what to say to her.

C : Well, it's up to you, but I wouldn't worry about it. Just make some small talk. Hey, Lucy. How's it going?

L : Oh, hi, Craig. I haven't seen you around lately. What's up?

C : Oh, not too much. You know, just hanging out, trying to stay cool.

L : Oh, so have I. It's so hot these days, isn't it?

C : It really is ... so ... Lucy ... How are your classes going?

L : Not too bad, but I can't seem to study. Maybe it's the heat.

C : It must be. Neither can I. Oh, by the way, Lucy, this is Ben. He's an old friend of mine. He just got back from Egypt.

L : Oh, really? That's interesting. What did you get up to there?

B : Ahh, you know, the usual stuff. The pyramids, bazaars, boat trips on the Nile. Have you ever been?

L : No, but I'd like to go. I really love traveling.

B : Oh, so do I. I just wish I had the money to do it more often ... So ... how long have you known Craig?

L : Only a couple of months. I only see him in class. We're not really friends. Yourself?

B : We go back a long way together. We don't really keep in touch these days, though.

L : Uhhh, Ben, are you enjoying this party?

B : Not really, to tell you the truth.

L : Me, neither. Are you feeling up to going to some other place?

B : I'd really like to, but I have to stay. It's *my* party!

Unit 2

Listening Track 03

Jason, Diane, and William are talking about their career changes.

J = Jason D = Diane W = William

PART 1

J : Hi! My name is Jason. I'm 38 years old, and I used to work as an advertising executive in a big company. I had a nice office, and I made lots of money. You know, even though I had a high salary, I wasn't looking at the big picture. I wasn't happy with my life. I enjoyed my work less and less every year. By the time I quit, I hated my work. It was so stressful, and I just didn't have my heart in it anymore. I quit, moved to another city, and became a musician. I've always loved and wanted to play music. But I was always busy with my old job. Since I quit, I've been playing music every day. I've been playing in a band, and trying to get as many chances as I can to perform in local clubs.

PART 2

D : Hi there! My name is Diane and I used to work as a secretary. My job was OK, but I just wasn't interested in my work. My life felt empty, and I felt like I was wasting my time. I'd always wanted to own my own business. I saved my money, and bought a small coffee shop in the countryside. I have paintings in my coffee shop, and I also sell books. My customers love it. I've been enjoying the summers in this area, because the trees are so beautiful. My coffee shop has become a popular stopping place for drivers, and I've been doing good business. The most important thing is that my coffee shop makes me happy and I'm proud of my business. I've been feeling greater satisfaction with my life.

PART 3

W : I quit my job as a taxi driver. It was stressful for me, and I felt no satisfaction or pride in my work anymore. Since quitting my job, I've been studying to become veterinarian. Going to university after my son graduated felt very strange. My wife has been encouraging me, and has been wonderful about it all. I've been feeling very happy about my career change. I've always loved animals, and it's great to be working towards a career that really interests me.

Unit 3

Listening Track 05

Three people are talking about their personal problems.

D = Dominic B = Beth S = Sean

D : Hi, and welcome to the Middleborough Self-help Meeting. I'm glad you could make it. Everyone will have the opportunity tonight to share their stories. Who would like to go first?

B : I'd like to get my story off my chest by sharing it with everyone. Well, I've been suffering from acrophobia for many years now. It has really affected my life.

D : Does the fear of heights always get to you?

B : Well, I never used to be afraid of heights because I used to climb trees when I was young. Up until last year, I couldn't even look out of a 2nd story window. It was so scary.

D : Don't you live in a high-rise apartment now?

B : Yeah, that's right. I live on the 15th floor. Each morning, I make myself look out the window. I used to be so scared I'd cry. But now, I'm getting used to it. What about you, Dominic? How's your nail-biting habit?

D : I'm doing very well. As you know, I used to be a serious nail-biter. My girlfriend said she wouldn't marry me until I stopped biting my nails. Well, that was a hard pill to swallow, so I told her she should get used to it, but she still refused to marry me.

B : So, have you stopped?

D : Almost. I started putting bad-tasting cream on my nails to stop me from biting them. But I'm getting used to the horrible flavor. I think I'll have to try something else.

B : Good luck, Dominic.

D : Thanks, Beth. What about you, Sean? You're new here. Do you want to open up and share your story?

S : I suppose. But I feel really stupid. It's embarrassing pouring your heart out to a group of strangers.

D : Don't be embarrassed, Sean. We're here to help and support each other.

S : Ah, OK. Well, I'm afraid of spiders. I've always had a problem with hairy things. I used to be afraid of mice. My kids had pet mice, so I had to overcome my fear of them. I'm used to them now, but I just can't overcome my fear of spiders.

B : What happens when you see a spider?

S : Well, I always used to scream and run away. But now I freeze, I can't move at all. All I can see are their long hairy legs and hairy bodies. I start to sweat and breathe rapidly. Then I feel dizzy. I've even fainted!

D : It sounds like you have a panic attack when you see a spider.

B : Hey, Sean! What's that crawling up your leg? Is that a spider?

S : Aaaaaaghhhhhhhhhhh!!!!!!!

Unit 4

Listening Track 06

David, Robert, and Beth are talking about their leisure preferences on a radio show.

H = Host D = David R = Robert B = Beth

H : Welcome back to "Putting fun back into your life." I'm Dan Ryan. Let's go right to your calls. David in Walnut Creek, California. You're on the air.

D : Thanks for taking my call. Dan, I founded an Internet company and was a millionaire at 28. But last year I sold it. Selling my company was the best choice I ever made.

H : I hear you. What do you do now?

D : Now, at 36, I'm trying the slow life. I live with my grandmother in a retirement condo.

H : Mm, what's that like?

D : Well, watching slow pitch softball is great. Last night my grandma's team ran away with the game, 7-0. You know, the old folks laugh at my hanging out at the swimming pool. But, hey, they enjoy playing Scrabble with me.

H : Will, uh, this be permanent for you?

D : Well, I may go back to working. But for now relaxing and playing bingo is just fine.

H : David, best of luck. Let's go to Robert in York, Pennsylvania.

R : Thanks for having me on. I'm a minister and love my work. But bowling is my second love. I bowl daily.

H : Bowling is a cool sport. Uh, our producer, Charles told me you motorcycle on weekends, too.

R : Motorcycling is my third great love. Even shopping for motorcycles is fun. The salesman says "This is a very fast, powerful bike. By the way, what kind of work do you do?" "I'm a minister," I say. "Oh, it's a very SAFE bike too," he says.

H : Great story. Robert, thanks for the call. We go to Beth, a chef in Marietta, Georgia. Now, Beth, you skydive, don't you?

B : Dan, skydiving is my passion. Running triathlons keeps me busy, too.

H : Uh, a triathlon has what? Swimming, biking, and running ...?

B : You got it. You swim 2 kilometers, bike 90 kilometers and run 21 kilometers.

H : I'm exhausted from even thinking about it. Beth, can you hold during our break?

B : Sure can.

H : We'll talk more. And, later on, "Does playing video games raise your IQ?" Stay tuned.

Unit 5

Listening Track 07

Helen is talking to Brad about some problems she is having with their relationship.

H = Helen B = Brad

H : How long have we been going out, Brad?

B : Uhhh, I'm not really too sure. I think it's been about a year and a half.

H : Actually, it's been twenty months exactly. I wish you were more romantic sometimes.

B : Oh, here we go. I hope you're not going to start with all that again, are you?

H : I keep bringing it up because I want you to understand how important things like that are to me, Brad. I've just about had it!

B : What's that supposed to mean?

H : Think about it. Last month, you forgot my birthday. On Valentine's Day, you didn't even get me a card.

B : I can't remember everything. I'm a busy guy.

H : I always hoped for someone more sensitive. I want someone who is considerate and caring. I'm sorry, Brad, but you're none of those things.

B : I hope you're not breaking up with me, Helen! I know I haven't been a good boyfriend in the last few months. I wish I could change, but I don't know how!

H : I hope to be married within two years, but I'm not sure that you're the right guy for me anymore.

B : I didn't realize I was so terrible.

H : You're not terrible, Brad. You have a lot of good points. You're kind and you've got a great sense of humor, but it's not enough.

B : Just tell me what I should do. I really want this to work, Helen.

H : Well, I wish you wouldn't drink so much. In fact, I want you to stop completely.

B : Stop drinking!

H : Secondly, I don't want you to play football anymore. It takes up too much of your time.

B : But I love football.

H : Also, I want you to start dressing better. I hope to take you out shopping with me so I can choose your clothes.

B : But I like my clothes.

H : Finally, I want you to spend more time with my family. It's important for you to get close to them.

B : But you know I don't get along with your mother.

H : It's time to start. I know it's a lot to ask, Brad, but do you think you can do it?

B : Helen, do you think if I did all those things it would make you happy?

H : ...

Unit 6

Listening Track 09

You will hear three TV commercials.

Commercial #1

H = Husband W = Wife A = Announcer

W : Honey, have you been exercising more?

H : No. Why do you ask?

W : You look good. You look younger. You look like a new man.

H : Ah, that's because of Wham Blamo's incredible new hair tonic. It will actually make your hair grow back!

W : I can't believe it. I mean, I could go for that, but does it really work?

H : It's true. I just splash a little on each day. It feels refreshing on my head.

W : It smells good, too. It smells like men's cologne.

H : Hey, let's go on a romantic weekend and leave the kids with your mother.

W : Yes, I'd love to.

A : Buy *Healing wind*, and it'll grow on you.

Commercial #2

W = Woman F = Friend A = Announcer

W : Hey, ready to go running?

F : I'm not in the mood for it. I feel really tired.

W : Try this new drink!

F : That sounds strange. It sounds like a glass of cola. I'm on a diet, you know.

W : Don't worry! You can drink this, and stay on your diet at the same time. It won't make you gain weight.

F : Not another diet drink! The last one I tried really turned my stomach.

W : Just try it!

F : It smells like a glass of wine. What is it?

W : It's called *Sensual*. *Sensual* is a new high-energy diet drink.

F : Oh my ...! It tastes like chocolate, and I feel great! What a fantastic drink!

W : Are you ready to go running?

F : Of course! Let's go!

A : Good taste, almost no calories, and it gives you the energy you need ... It's *Sensual*.

Commercial #3

T = Traveler N = Non-native speaker A = Announcer P = Pocket translator

T : Hi! Excuse me, but you look like a local person.

N : Sorry ... no ... English.

T : I am an American. Could you please tell me the way to the nearest train station?

N : No English ...

T : Let me try again. Could you please tell ...?

N : Moment ...

T : What's that? That looks like a calculator.

P : I am an *English Away* pocket translator. I fit the bill for any English translation. How may I help you?

T : What a useful device! It sounds so natural and clear.

P : Why, thank you. The train station is down this street. Turn left at the intersection, and you'll see it after that. You can't miss it.

A : *English Away* for any time that you need more English.

Unit 7

Listening Track 10

Mike is on a bus and a stranger wants to tell him a story.

M = Mike S = Stranger

S : I'd like to tell you about something I know. You seem like a good person and it's important.

M: Oh ... really? That's very ...

S : A friend of mine said that he had some information about UFOs. He told me that it was a big story. Big ...!

M: I see. Why did I take the bus?

S : My friend sent me a computer disk in the mail with a letter. The letter said that the government had found out about him.

M: The government? What?

S I phoned my friend, but his landlady said that he had moved out. I said that it was impossible, but she said she didn't care. They killed him — I'm sure of it!

M: Who do you mean? Who are they? Who killed him?

S : Them ... The people we don't know about!

M: What are you talking about?

S : Last week I climbed a hill near one of our air-force bases. I saw our pilots flying UFOs!

M: You ... What?

S : That's not all. I saw Elvis Presley!

M: Are you telling me that you saw the King of Rock and Roll, alive, and on an air force base with UFOs?

S : He was the air-force commander! The government must have needed him for some reason. That's why they faked his death.

M: Well ... that's very interesting.

S : I don't know how long I have. Some Men in Black visited my apartment last night.

M: Men in Black?

S : I think they work for the government.

M: OK, that doesn't surprise me.

S : They suggested that I stop my research. They said that my friend had ignored them. They told me that I shouldn't make the same mistake.

M: Do you think your life is in danger?

S : Exactly! This is my stop! Remember what I told you. It's a conspiracy, and people have to know the truth!

M: OK. I hate taking the bus.

Unit 8

Listening Track 12

Bob has just met Jodi at the mall by chance.

B = Bob J = Jodi L = Liam

B : Hey Jodi, what are you doing?

J : Oh, hi, Bob. I'm waiting for someone but there's been a mix-up and they're late, so I'm just people watching.

B : Do you mind if I join you?

J : No, of course not. Be my guest.

B : I don't recognize anyone. I think all of the people here are from out of town.

J : Yeah, I think you're right.

B : Hey, look at that guy over there. I'm positive he's one of them.

J : Hey, I'm one of them too.

B : Really? Looks like I've put my foot in my mouth again.

J : No, just kidding but what makes you think he's one of them?

B : It's obvious. Just look at his body language.

J : What about his body language?

B : Can't you see? All of the ones I've met use a lot of hand gestures when they talk.

J : What are you talking about? Most people use body language when they talk. What's different?

B : It's just a little different to most of the guys I know.

J : Few of the guys you know are worth knowing.

B : Very funny. Okay, take a look at his appearance.

J : He looks just like a lot of other guys. In fact, he's more handsome than most guys.

B : Exactly, and that's so typical. What about his gold necklace, bleach blond hair and his sleeveless shirt? Every one of them looks like that.

J : You're not thinking straight. I know some famous rappers who have a similar look and none of them are like that.

B : But he's wearing an earring, too.

J : Look, Bob, just because he's wearing an earring, it doesn't mean he's like that and even if he is, what's the problem?

B : Look, I think we're getting our wires crossed here. A few of my colleagues are like that and I don't have a problem with them.

J : Then why haven't I ever seen you hanging around with any of them?

B : Just because you've never seen me with any of them, it doesn't mean I don't know any. I've got nothing against them, I just don't like it when they want to get married and adopt kids.

J : You're on the wrong track. Very few want to do that and anyway they have the right to live like anyone else.

B : Maybe they do, but I don't want to know about it.

J : That's what every straight guy says.

B : Look, Jodi, I think he's coming over here.

J : Maybe he heard what you said about him.

B : Yeah, and he's big, too. I think I really messed up this time.

L : Excuse me. Are you Jodi?

J : Yes, I am, do I know you?

L : I'm Liam. I was supposed to meet you for a date tonight.

J : Hi, Liam, how's it going? Oh, by the way, this is my gay friend Bob. Oh sorry, slip of the tongue. I meant to say my great friend Bob.

Unit 9

Listening Track 13

A TV reporter is talking about a trial for a famous actor.

A = Anchor R = Reporter

A : Now, we go to our reporter, Susan Spheres. What can you tell us, Susan?

R: I'm in front of the courthouse, where Johnny Liebling's trial is taking place.

A: It looks like there are a lot of people there.

R : That's right, Walter. Johnny Liebling has many fans and is adored by millions of young women around the world. He is often considered by many to be the next Brad Pitt.

A : It sounds like there's a lot of support for the young Hollywood actor.

R : He's loved by his fans, and this is why the trial is closed to the general public. People aren't allowed into the courtroom unless they are involved with the trial.

A : Please explain what led up to this trial.

R : His sudden rise to fame was soon followed by his breakup with his fiancée, Nicole Lamont. His friends were concerned, and he was said to be having trouble keeping his cool, but no one knew that he had become an alcoholic.

A : I heard a report that a director had criticized him recently. He said that he was getting carried away at times and that he needed to get his act together.

R : That's right. Before his arrest, he was heard arguing with that director, and was seen breaking chairs and leaving the set of his current movie.

A : Why was he charged with a criminal offence?

R : Well, the director's car was stolen from the film studio. It was later ruined in an accident, and Johnny Liebling was found in the car.

A : Wasn't Mr. Liebling injured by the crash?

R : Not seriously, Walter. He was arrested by police and was given medical attention.

A : Has Mr. Liebling made a statement about the event?

R : Yes, he has. A more levelheaded Johnny Liebling offered his apologies to his director and all his coworkers. He said that he was deeply affected by what happened, and hopes to win his battle with alcoholism.

A : It seems like there are some people coming out of the courthouse now.

R : One moment ... Yes, we were just told that the trial has finished. A light sentence was decided on: Johnny Liebling will need to pay money for all the damage he caused, as well as a fine to the city.

A : Is that all?

R : One moment ... He is also expected to go for rehabilitation. Yes, the jury has decided that he must enter a facility for the treatment of alcoholism.

A : I imagine the film producers won't be happy about that. Thanks for that intriguing report, Susan.

R : Thank you, Walter.

A : Now, let's look at the weather ...

Unit 10

Listening Track 14

Nigel is a reporter interviewing people for a radio show about community volunteer work.

N = Nigel R = Raynor C = Clive

Dialogue 1

N : It's a beautiful day here today and I'm talking to musician, Raynor Hill, who is about to do her first parachute jump. Hello, Raynor, how are you feeling?

R : It's hard to say, Nigel. Obviously, I've got the jitters but I've done a lot of preparation so I'm also fairly upbeat.

N : How high is it?

R : You mean how high will I be jumping from?

N : Right.

R : It's about 12,000 feet, I believe.

N : There are a lot of people who must think you're mad. Why are you doing this?

R : It's simple, Nigel. I'm raising money for kids with leukemia. With the donations we collect, we plan to send the patients on a wonderful vacation to Disneyland.

N : How does it work exactly?

R : Well, there are 20 of us altogether. Each of us asks everyone we know to sponsor us with whatever they can afford. If we complete the jump ... and live, we collect the money and make our contribution to charity.

Dialogue 2

N : Excuse me, Clive. Do you have a moment? There are a couple of questions I'd like to ask you.

C : Sure, Nigel. It's pretty quiet here at the moment.

N : Do you work here?

C : Yes, but I'm a volunteer. I work as an electrician in my real job.

N : Why do you do it?

C : What? You mean volunteer?

N : That's right.

C : Well, there is a tradition in my family of volunteering. I get a lot of satisfaction from it and I love animals. It's a wonderful thing to volunteer for anything.

N : And what exactly does this organization do?

C : It's a shelter for animals. We mostly deal with cats and dogs that have been mistreated and abandoned. There is a dog here, for example, we found this morning, that had been beaten and left for dead on a garbage dump. What kind of person would do that?

N : How long does it take to find a new owner?

C : Well, that's where we come in. It depends how quickly we can nurse the dog back to health. Usually, they have some psychological problems due to the abuse, so we spend time with them to regain their trust of humans. If there are no complications, maybe six to ten weeks.

N : Thanks, Clive, and keep up the good work.

Unit 11

Listening Track 16

Three people are speaking about their friendships.

Monologue 1

Ramsay and I have been best friends for about eight years. I'll never forget the first time we met. I had recently broken off my engagement and I was feeling low. A mutual friend introduced us and I remember Ramsay's reaction. He was happy and jumping with joy to make a new friend. From that moment, he became my best buddy. Ramsay started coming to work with me about seven years ago. I work as a truck driver, so it can be pretty lonely on the road especially when the truck breaks down and I have to wait for hours for help. I thought I could do with some company. Ramsay was also lonely and unhappy staying at home all day. So I asked him if he wanted to join me. He loves being on the road, and it's nice to have someone to talk to. At that time we were helping each other out, so the proverb "A friend in need is a friend indeed" described our friendship. And Ramsay's such a good listener. Ramsay's got a great personality. He's friendly and outgoing. People are always walking up to him to say hi. Because of him, I've met a lot of new people. Ramsay is also loyal. He has stuck with me through thick and thin. I don't know what I'd do without him.

Monologue 2

I moved to this neighborhood about four years ago. I had graduated from university and started a new job in a new city. I didn't know anyone, so I was feeling a little scared and lonely. One day, there was a knock at my door. It was Alison, my next door neighbor, she was welcoming me to the neighborhood. We had a cup of tea and a chat that day, and that was the beginning of our friendship. Alison has called in regularly since then. Alison has had a lot of life experiences. She was married and had a couple of children. She spent about 35 years living in foreign countries with her family because her husband worked as a foreign diplomat. Alison has told me many wonderful and amazing stories about her adventures overseas. She's full of good advice also. When I broke up with my boyfriend, she was there for me saying "A problem shared is a problem halved," and when I needed some advice doing up my house, she gave me her opinions. Alison and I both have a really good sense of humor, so we spend a lot of time laughing about different things. We get along so well, I'm so glad Alison knocked on my door that day.

Monologue 3

Yuki is like a sister to me. We have been great friends since our children were young. Actually, we met because of our children — they attended the same kindergarten. We started chatting one day and discovered that we have similar interests. We both love reading mystery novels. So we read the same books, then she calls me up or I call her up and discuss the characters and plots. Yuki also has a passion for gardening, and so do I. We spend hours helping in each other's garden. We talk about everything as we work. She tells me about her childhood growing up in the hustle-bustle of the city, and I tell her about my life growing up in the country. Even though our backgrounds are different, we share the same philosophy. We've put a lot of time and effort into our relationship because a good friend is sooner lost than won. There are many things we can do without in life, but we can't do without true friends.

Unit 12

Listening Track 17

Three talk show guests are talking about "lookism".

H = Host N = Narrator C = Carl B1 = Becky B2 = Byker

H : Welcome, welcome. Thanks for joining us. Before we talk to the guests, I wanna show this Shooters promotional video. Take a look ...

N : Every day is a beach party at Shooters. Beer and burgers. 60's surf music. Hula dancing. And the beautiful Shooters' bikini waitresses — Wow! It seems just like Hawaii!

H : Carl Russell thinks Shooters is guilty of "lookism" because it won't hire male waiters. Welcome, Carl.

C : Thank you.

H : Now, I believe "Beauty is only skin deep." But "Shooters" is, um, a "theme" restaurant. Bikinis, beach parties, uh ...

C : I realize that, but I'm arguing that they can hire waiters. Their whole Hawaiian Hula thing is really just "lookism." I mean, who doesn't notice that the waitresses are only thin, blond-haired types?

H : I hear you're taking Shooters to court over this. Correct?

C : Yeah. It's a $4 million court case, but I doubt I'll win.

H : Let's now talk to Becky Sharp, a Shooters' manager. Welcome, Becky.

B1: Anthony, I understand Carl's viewpoint, but looks are deceiving. I've hired lots of waitresses with black hair, red hair ... all kinds of appearan-

C : Yeah, I bet none of them weigh over 55 kilos. And be-

B1: That is not tr-

C : And, and, and ...

B1: Wait, wait, let me ...

C : And, they, they ...

H : One at a time, one at a time. Becky ...

B1: Shooters is just a theme restaurant. Everyone knows that true beauty comes from within.

H : We're joined now by Dr. Byker Hoffman. She's a sociologist who found out that "lookism" is a big problem in other industries too. She researched lookism in hiring by visiting over 100 Cromley and Fincher clothing stores. And ... What did you find?

B2: Cromley and Fincher considers itself a preppie clothing store, and in the stores I visited over 75% of the male clerks were tall, blond, football-player types.

H : We gotta take a break. Later, we'll hear about the $40 million court case against Cromley and Fincher. We'll be right back.

Unit 1

Small talk Related Expressions

★ **long time no see** = used to say that a long time has passed since you last saw someone
Wow, **long time no see**! What have you been doing since high school?

★ **How about ...?** = a way to ask what someone thinks about a topic
How about the weather lately? Hasn't it been crazy?

★ **Catch you later** = a casual way of saying 'good-bye'
I've got to go now. **Catch you later**.

★ **Take it easy** = an informal way to say 'good-bye'
It was nice to meet you. **Take it easy**.

Weather Related Expressions

★ **cool down** = to become colder
The weather man said that it should **cool down** by Thursday.

★ **roll in** = to approach from a distance
Can you see those clouds **rolling in**? I think it's going to rain soon.

★ **rain cats and dogs** = to rain very hard
It's **raining cats and dogs** right now.

★ **die down** = to reduce in strength
The snowstorm **died down** enough that we could go skiing.

More Expressions

Write down any new expressions you learned in class.

Unit 2

Business Related Expressions

★ **do good business** = to do well in business
My coffee shop has become a popular stopping place for drivers, and I'm doing good business.

★ **dog eat dog world** = a very competitive state of affairs
The electronics retail market is often considered to be a dog eat dog world.

★ **go out of business** = to fail in business and have to close
We worked hard, but in the end the economy was against us. We're going out of business.

★ **rat race** = a fierce struggle for success in business
Jason decided that he had enough of the rat race, and quit to become a musician.

Stress Related Expressions

★ **stress someone out** = to cause someone stress
Shopping for clothes can really stress me out.

★ **under a lot of pressure** = facing an urgent state of affairs
I'm under a lot of pressure at work these days.

★ **pile up** = to have a lot of something, to which more is added
My family troubles are really piling up on me lately.

★ **can't take it** = not be able to tolerate something or someone
I can't take it anymore! Turn the music down.

More Expressions

Write down any new expressions you learned in class.

Unit 3

Fear Related Expressions

★ **a bundle of nerves** = very nervous, tense, or worried
My daughter is taking her English test today. She's a bundle of nerves.

★ **make someone's blood run cold** = to make someone very scared or shocked
The look in the prisoner's eyes made my blood run cold.

★ **have butterflies in someone's stomach** = to feel very nervous
Dong Min felt like he had butterflies in his stomach. He was really worried about giving presentation.

★ **afraid of someone's own shadow** = very nervous or easily frightened
I've never met someone who is easily scared. You're afraid of your own shadow!

Optimism Related Expressions

★ **not the end of the world** = it's not reason enough to lose hope
Losing your girlfriend isn't the end of the world. You will meet someone else soon.

★ **keep someone's fingers crossed** = to hope for good luck
Keep your fingers crossed that we can find a place to park.

★ **look on the bright side** = said to someone to get them to focus on the positive side
Look on the bright side, at least you have your health.

★ **every cloud has a silver lining** = something good can come from a bad situation
I'm sorry that things have gone badly, but remember 'every cloud has a silver lining'.

More Expressions

Write down any new expressions you learned in class.

Unit 4

Relaxing Related Expressions

★ **take a nap** = to sleep for a short time
I try to take a nap every afternoon.

★ **take a break** = to rest by stopping work or doing something relaxing
We've been working hard all week. Let's take a break.

★ **have free time** = to have little or no work; free time
Whenever Jang Hoon has free time, he likes to go hiking.

★ **pass the time** = to spend time relaxing
You should try reading to pass the time while we wait.

Expressions Derived From *Sport*

★ **kick off** = to begin (from football)
The Cannes film festival will kick off next week.

★ **par for the course** = typical; what is to be expected (from golf)
Is a $7.00 cup of coffee par for the course in New York?

★ **hit someone below the belt** = something that is not fair (from boxing)
The politician's ad campaign really hits his opponent below the belt.

★ **neck and neck** = close in a competition (from horse racing)
Robert and Beth were neck and neck in the contest for the promotion.

More Expressions

Write down any new expressions you learned in class.

Unit 5

Dating Related Expressions

★ **go out** = to date
Helen has been going out with Brad for more than two years.

★ **break up** = to end a romantic relationship
Are you breaking up with me?

★ **Mr/Ms. Right** = the perfect mate for someone
I know I'm not Mr. Right, but I thought we were happy!

★ **put the past behind someone** = to try and work out any problems and forget about them
Carol told her Rene that she just wants to put the past behind them.

Argument Related Expressions

★ **bring up** = to mention or talk about someone or something
I keep bringing up your ex-girlfriend because I want you to stop calling her!

★ **have had it** = to be tired or disgusted with someone or something
I've had it with your drinking. You need to stop.

★ **start with that again** = to mention something again
I hope you're not going to start with that again. I said I would wash the dishes later!

★ **You can say that again** = said to someone to mean 'I completely agree'
When she said that we were done, I said "You can say that again!"

More Expressions

Write down any new expressions you learned in class.

Unit 6

Gratitude Related Expressions

★ **owe it to someone** = to be in someone's debt
I owe it to my family and friends for being so supportive.

★ **count someone's lucky stars** = to be indebted to someone
We can count our lucky stars that we weren't on that plane that crashed.

★ **hand it to someone** = to give some praise for something someone have done
You have to hand it to Ms. Kim. She was the one who made this deal possible.

★ **hats off to** = to congratulate someone for something they have done
Hats off to Bryan. He scored higher than anyone in the school on the SATs.

Persuasion Related Expressions

★ **charm the pants off someone** = to be very charming and persuasive
Paul is really persuasive. He could charm the pants off anyone.

★ **like getting blood from a stone** = difficult or impossible to get something from
Trying to persuade him to work is like getting blood from a stone.

★ **sell ice to the Eskimo** = used to say that someone can accomplish very difficult tasks
Min Ji is quite a sales person. She could sell ice to the Eskimo.

★ **dog and pony show** = a show or event organized to persuade people of something (negative)
The tour was part of the dog and pony show put on by the government to encourage tourism.

More Expressions

Write down any new expressions you learned in class.

Unit 7

Authority Related Expressions

★ **bulldoze into** = to force someone into doing something
He felt that he was being bulldozed into telling his story.

★ **force someone's hand** = to make someone do something unwillingly, or sooner than planned
The reporter's questions had forced Sang Min's hand, so he revealed the location of the spaceship.

★ **the corridors of power** = the highest levels of government
The matter of contacting the aliens is being discussed in the corridors of power right now!

★ **crack the whip** = to use authority to get someone to obey, usually under threat
Every once in a while I need to crack the whip to make sure people get the work done.

Behavior Related Expressions

★ **bury someone's head in the sand** = refuse to face an unpleasant situation by pretending it doesn't exist
It's no good burying your head in the sand. We need to address the problem.

★ **dig someone's own grave** = to do something which causes your own downfall
If you drop of university this year, you'll be digging your own grave.

★ **go too far** = to do something extreme or unacceptable
Stealing is bad, but stealing from the poor is going too far!

★ **go off the rails** = to be out of control and behave in an unacceptable manner
Given the stress that many people are under nowadays, it's surprising that more people don't go off the rails.

More Expressions

Write down any new expressions you learned in class.

Unit 8

Description related Expressions

★ **cold-hearted** = lacking sympathy or feeling; unkind
He never listens to me when I talk about my feelings. He's so cold-hearted.

★ **open-minded** = receptive to new ideas
I always found my boss to be very open-minded when it comes to ways to improve worker morale.

★ **level-headed** = having common sense and sound judgment; sensible
I trust her judgment. She's very level-headed.

★ **two-faced** = deceitful or hypocritical
I can't trust them. They say one thing to me and another to my friends. They're so two-faced.

Embarrassment Related Expressions

★ **put someone's foot in someone's mouth** = to say something stupid or insulting, and then regret saying it
I really put my foot in my mouth when I told Matthew that all blondes were dumb. Mathew is blond!

★ **save face** = to preserve someone's dignity or image
In a situation where you are obviously wrong it's better to save face by admitting it.

★ **be put on the spot** = to be in an awkward position
Becky was put on the spot when she couldn't answer her student's question.

★ **make an ass out of someone** = to cause someone to look foolish
If he keeps up this childish behavior he'll make an ass out of himself.

More Expressions

Write down any new expressions you learned in class.

Unit 9

Law Related Expressions

★ **long arm of the law** = the extent to which the authority of the law extends
Johnny fled to the Cayman Islands, hoping to escape the **long arm of the law**.

★ **catch someone red-handed** = to catch someone while doing something wrong or illegal
I **caught my sister red-handed**. She was going through the things in my closet!

★ **paper trail** = written or documented evidence that serves as proof of someone's actions
The police found a **paper trail** which lead to the arrest of the politician.

★ **toe the line** = to obey the rules; to accept the principles of a group or organization
If you want to continue to study here, you will need to **toe the line**.

Support Related Expressions

★ **back someone up** = to support someone
I know that he left the house around 10:00am. **Back me up** on this, Sam!

★ **go to bat for someone** = to defend or argue for someone
Thanks for **going to bat for me** with the boss. If it wasn't for you I might have been fired.

★ **stand behind** = to strongly believe in and support
I don't care what he said. I **stand behind** what I said.

★ **not have a leg to stand on** = to have no reasonable support
I don't know how Brad plans to get out of the traffic fine. He doesn't **have a leg to stand on**.

More Expressions

Write down any new expressions you learned in class.

Unit 10

Safety Related Expressions

★ **throw caution to the wind** = to stop caring about possible dangers and risks
He threw caution to the wind and decided to try skydiving.

★ **look before you leap** = something said when advising someone to think carefully when doing something
Don't decide on a college right away. Look before you leap.

★ **be on the safe side** = to avoid taking risks
To be on the safe side, I suggest that we invest in gold.

★ **be in safe hands** = to be looked after by a reliable person or organization
He'll look after the children while you're gone. They'll be in safe hands.

Cooperation Related Expressions

★ **pull together** = to work together for a common purpose
If we pull together we can do anything.

★ **put our/their heads together** = to cooperate in order to find a solution to a problem
We can put our heads together to find a way to help those in poverty.

★ **bend over backwards** = to make an extra effort to help or satisfy someone
Gi Won bent over backwards to make sure her student passed, but he failed anyway.

★ **a real sport** = someone who cooperates or does a favor willingly
You're a real sport for helping me move to my new place this weekend.

More Expressions

Write down any new expressions you learned in class.

Unit 11

Happiness Related Expressions

★ **be all smiles** = to be very happy
Marcy was all smiles when she learned her son had made the hockey team.

★ **be in seventh heaven** = to be extremely happy
You'll be in seventh heaven if you win the lottery tomorrow.

★ **make someone's day** = to make someone very happy
It really made my day when she told me I looked great.

★ **feel blue** = to be very sad or depressed
She's feeling a little blue today. Her boyfriend flew back home yesterday.

Problem Solving Related Expressions

★ **get to the bottom of** = to finally find an explanation for something
He couldn't get to the bottom of things until he knew how the robbers entered the vault.

★ **two heads are better than one** = two people can find a solution more easily than one person
Two heads are better than one when it comes to dealing with complex problems.

★ **iron out** = to resolve a problem; to reach an agreement
They need to iron out their differences if they want the relationship to grow.

★ **do the trick** = to have the desired result; to be an adequate solution
The leaky pipe could be a problem, but placing duct tape over the leak should do the trick.

More Expressions

Write down any new expressions you learned in class.

Unit 12

Appearance Related Expressions

★ **a face (that) only a mother could love** = used to say that someone is very ugly or unattractive
That poor guy has a face that only a mother could love.

★ **look like a million bucks** = to look or feel extremely good
With the new hairstyle, he looked like a million bucks.

★ **as fresh as a daisy** = used to describe someone as lively and attractive
I met Giovanna the other day. She looked as fresh as a daisy.

★ **never/not a hair out of place** = used to say that someone's appearance is perfect
She is always dressed well – never a hair out of place.

Patience Related Expressions

★ **hold someone's horses** = to be patient (usually used as a command)
Hold your horses! I'm not ready to leave yet.

★ **sit tight** = to wait patiently and see how a situation develops
They sat tight on the side of the mountain until the storm passed.

★ **try someone's patience** = to cause someone to become impatient
These constant interruptions of yours are really trying my patience.

★ **jump the gun** = to do something before the proper time; to act impatiently
Ji Yeon jumped the gun when she tried claimed victory before the election results came in.

More Expressions

Write down any new expressions you learned in class.